Keeping Warm and Dry

by Harry Roberts

Published by

Stone Wall Press
1241 30th Street N.W.,
Washington, D.C. 20007

Distributed by

Stackpole Books
Cameron & Kelker Streets,
Harrisburg, Pennsylvania 17105

Publishers disclaimer:
The products and processes referred to in this book reflect the sole opinion of the author and not the publisher or any other party or person.

cover photography credits: top left by Glenn D. Chambers, Ducks Unlimited.
top right by Tim Irwin, Uniphoto, Inc.
bottom, courtesy of American Hiking Society

cover preparation by Kim F. Hasten
interior art and design by Jerry Burnett

Library of Congress Catalog Card No. 82-061003
ISBN 0-913276-40-5

Printed in the United States of America

Table of Contents

Dedication

It takes a lot of people to make a book. I may do the writing, but everybody else in our large and oftentimes wacky household helps to keep me alive with their encouragement—and sometimes by the simple fact that they restrain themselves from strangling me. So, to Molly, Kathy, Cindy, Larry, Nathaniel and Jared — many, many thanks and much, much love.

But that's not a dedication. This is:

This book is for Skipper and Big Gene. I mean, we're talking fox, Jack. And don't you forget it.

Introduction:
Ed and Charlie

December third. Snow on the ground, even where the sun could get at it. Back in the woods it's six inches deep. At 4:30 in the morning there's a nip to the Adirondack air that sets the fillings in your molars to tingling. The black four-wheeler swings off the Interstate at the Route 9 exit for Pottersville, and predictably pulls into the Black Bear Diner. Ed and Charlie, stocky middle-aged men in red and black checked wool hunting clothing, climb out of the truck and walk inside.

"Jeez, Eddie, I could eat a wolf. Damn, it's cold up here."

"Yeah, so could I. Place is full. Hell, let's grab some coffee and doughnuts. We'll be fine. Live off our fat, hey, buddy?"

They sit, straddling the stools, and chat with the waitress. Three cups of coffee and three doughnuts later, they leave.

"Hey, Charlie, that hit the spot. I was getting sleepy riding. Guess I shouldn't have gone over to my brother-in-law's place last night."

"Uh-huh. We stayed home. Drank some beer and watched the fights on cable."

"Well, let's get on the road. Minerva's not that far away. Get there just about in time."

A half-hour later, the four-wheeler comes to the end of a short dirt road, and Ed and Charlie slide out. Ed opens the tailgate. They both take their rifles out of cases, slip on bright orange plastic vests, don orange caps, and leave.

The country out of Minerva isn't the steep, craggy Adirondacks of the downstater's dreams. But it's rugged, strewn with wind thrown trees and laced with hills and valleys. As far as walking goes, it'd make a good NFL training camp.

"Hey Charlie, where in hell are we going?"

"Okay. We'll go up this way along this ridge above Minerva Brook. Then we'll pick up this trail and head sorta north up to this

1

little bump. There's some open ledges on it, and you can see a lot of country from it. Then we'll just work the country around until we get something."

"Sounds good to me. Got a map or something? I've never been here."

"Naah. Know this place like the back of my hand. Hell, we come up here every summer. Ever since Johnny was three we've been coming here."

They walk on silently for twenty minutes, staring intently from side to side.

"Hmmm. No tracks. Snow's gotta be a few days old."

"Naah. Never are, right here."

"Mmmm."

They walk on in silence.

"Hey, Charlie, where's that damn trail?"

"Ahhh, oughta be along in here soon."

Fifteen minutes later, Charlie stops and looks back over his shoulder. He turns to Ed and grins ruefully.

"Jeez, the place looks different in the snow, you know? Musta walked right on by the trail. Let's go back. Plenty of day left, Eddie."

Twenty minutes later they found the trail, dropped off the ridge, and crossed a boggy area, the remnants of an old beaver pond on a tributary to Minerva Brook. Both men broke through the thin ice several times, but it wasn't until the last few steps that Eddie went in over the top of his left boot.

"Whoa! Man, that's cold! Aw, what the hell. I'll live."

"Boy, that's a bummer. Wanna change your socks?"

"Naw. Sock'll dry. No problem. Hey, it almost felt good. I was working up a sweat back there!"

They skirted two more ridges. Not much elevation change. Scarcely over two hundred feet. But a hard two hundred. Steep, even slippery in spots. By the time they got to the base of the bald-topped knob, Charlie's face was dripping with sweat.

The ascent of the knob was hampered by fallen trees across the trail, and some very slick spots where the path crossed some shelving rock. At one point they were grabbing tree branches and hoisting themselves up. When they finally reached the top, both men were sweating heavily.

"Phew. Eddie, I guess I gotta lose some weight. Man, that was a lot rougher than when I last did it. Must have lost five pounds coming up there."

"Yeah. Let's catch a breather here for a minute."

2

"Sounds good to me."

Ed and Charlie sat down on the trunk of a downed tree in the grey, chilly dawn. From afar came the sound of two quick shots. Then silence. They nodded to each other. Ed gave Charlie the thumbs-up sign.

"Okay. That'll get them stirred up and moving. Let's go out to the ledges and scout around. Mostly hardwoods up here. It was timbered way back, and then there was a burn. If anything's moving, we ought to be able to see it."

"Good idea, Ed. Gets chilly sitting here. How's that foot? Getting cold?"

"Naw. I put on a couple extra pairs of socks when I left the house. No problem. A little cold, that's all. Aah, you expect that, you know. Let's go."

They circled the knob, staring into the surrounding timber. The sun broke through the clouds timidly, casting a pale light with no warmth on the rugged countryside.

"Might turn out to be a good day after all. Hey, Eddie, did you hear a weather report? I forgot to listen last night."

"So did I. Guess it'll be okay. Hey, you know it's damn chilly up here. That little breeze just goes right through you. Let's drop off the ridge and hunt down below. Still hunt, you know. Keep moving and we'll warm up real quick."

The way down was rougher than the way up. Both men had to slide down virtually hand-over-hand from ledge to ledge. Neither slipped, but by the time they got to the valley, their clothing was covered with snow. They brushed each other off perfunctorily and started walking side by side, Charlie scanning to the left, Ed to the right. The going was rough. This was a valley only because it obviously wasn't a mountain.

"How's the foot doing, Eddie?"

"Okay. No problem. Damn hands are cold, though. Gloves got wet back there when we came off the knob. Damn. Thought I had some dry ones in my pocket, but I guess I don't. Sure thought I left a pair in the coat after last year, but I guess I took them out. How you doing?"

"Kind of chilly around the edges. Collar on the jacket's soaked. Feels like a wet blanket on my neck. It isn't all that late, but I'm getting hungry. Should have brought some sandwiches."

"I got a candy bar, I think." Eddie rummaged in the pockets of his heavy wool coat. "Yeah. Here it is. Grabbed it off the kitchen counter this morning. The kid'll yell like hell when he finds out the old man stole it out of his lunch."

"Naah. He'll blame it on his sister if he's like mine, you know."

"Hey, you're right." Eddie handed the chocolate bar to Charlie. "Want half, Ed?"

"No. Never eat when I hunt. Slows me down. Finish it off, Charlie."

They walked on. The wind came up smartly, reaching into the forest. Both men turned up the wet collars of their hunting coats against it, and unrolled the earmuffs on their caps.

"Damn earlappers are wet. Must have really worked up a sweat back there. Funny thing, Ed. I was sweating like a pig, but I'm still chilly. You think you'd be warm, you know."

"Yeah. Funny how things work sometimes."

They moved on in silence. A half-hour passed. Ed turned to Charlie. "Hey meathead, how you expect to get a shot with your right hand in your pocket?"

"Must have dropped a glove back there when I ate the candy bar. Thought I put it in my pocket, but I guess it fell out."

"Got another pair?"

"Nope. Thought about bringing some, but never got around to finding them. Hand's okay, though."

The wind rose. The sun dipped under a bank of clouds, not to return. Flakes of snow drifted it crisply. In another hour, Ed and Charlie were visibly shivering.

"Hey, Eddie, I'm getting cold as hell. Let's go back to the truck and warm up. Maybe go into Olmstedville and find some gloves. What you think?"

"Yeah. About time to eat, too. Nothing much moving. Yeah, let's go."

They turned and walked back the way they had come. The snow was falling harder now. You could see the build-up in their tracks and on the shoulders of their jackets. Eddie was moving heavily, slowly.

"What's the matter, Ed?"

"Damn foot doesn't work. You know, the one I got wet? Feels like a block of ice. Oh, it'll warm up. We about there?"

"Yeah. Coming up. The knob ought to be off on the left. Damn snow! Can't see anything."

"Think we passed it?"

"No. We'd have spotted our trail. I don't think it'd fill up with snow yet. Maybe it did. Ah, no sweat."

When they came to the place where Charlie had eaten the candy bar, there was enough snow accumulation that neither man saw Ed's

4

glove on the ground. They walked on. Both were shivering hard by now.

"Charlie, where in hell's the turnoff? We passed it. I know we did. Damn it, we've been out here for hours. We passed it long ago!"

"No we didn't. Hey, I know this country, don't I? I spent ten years up here."

"But that's two lousy weeks in summer, Charlie. We're lost, damn it. We'll never get back!"

"Hey, no problem. We just turn right, and we get to the ridge over the brook. Then we turn left to the truck."

"Let's do it. I know we passed that trail. We've been backtracking for hours."

They turned, heading for the ridge above Minerva Brook. The trail turnoff was still a half-hour's walk ahead of them, but by now their tracks were covered by the fast-falling snow. They headed in the right direction, but instead of skirting the little knobs, the new route took them over the top of two of them and right into the teeth of the wind. By the time they got to the ridge, Eddie was stumbling and staggering like he'd been on all-night pub crawl.

"Eddie, c'mon. Let's go. Here's the ridge. Here's the old tote road that we left the truck on. We're almost there."

"We're not there. We're lost. Gonna die out here," Eddie mumbled.

By the time they reached the truck, Charlie had to push Ed inside. Ed slumped in the seat, muttering under his breath. It took Charlie fully five minutes of fumbling with his keys to unlock his door. He couldn't rouse Ed to open it for him.

When Charlie got into the truck, he could barely get the key into the ignition. But soon heat was pouring out of the four-wheeler's oversized heater. Charlie, still shivering hard, managed to turn the truck around and head back to the highway. Ed was still slumped in the front seat, mumbling incoherently.

"Eddie! Eddie, dammit. C'mon. We're out. It's okay."

Ed didn't answer. He seemed no better when they got back to Pottersville and the Black Bear.

"Ed. Hey, buddy, we're here. Let's get a hot coffee and some food. Ed. Ed? Eddie?! What the hell's wrong!!"

Charlie stumbled into the warmth of the Black Bear, and asked the waitress if there was a doctor in town. He told her that his buddy had gotten really cold, and was dozing in the truck and wouldn't wake up. A slender, bearded young man, nursing a coffee at the end of the counter, got to his feet, shook Charlie, and said, "Let's go."

"Hey. What do you mean, fella? Lemme finish my coffee!"

"Look, dummy, your buddy's in trouble, and you ain't much better off. Let's go!"

He steered Charlie out of the Black Bear, piled him into the four-wheeler, and roared back up the road, turning into a house with a small sign in front that was obscured by the snow. The young man pounded on the door. "Hey Doc! Move it. Two of 'em. One's okay, sort of, but one's in real bad shape."

****

It happens that way sometimes. I know. I've been the skinny guy with the beard at the end of the counter in the Black Bear on a couple of occasions, and it's no fun.

It's even less fun for the guys who had to be herded, stumbling and incoherent, to the doctor's for emergency treatment. And none of it had to happen.

That's the shame of the whole thing. None of what happened to Ed and Charlie had to happen. The worst that should have happened was that the hunt itself was unsuccessful, and they got a bit chilly around the edges. Instead, Ed wound up in the Glens Falls hospital with severe hypothermia and a badly frostbitten foot. And Charlie was chilled and aching for days.

It bothers me to see this happen. And it happens so many times, all across the country. You don't need the rigors of a North Country winter for it to happen, either. A rainy 50° F day with a good, crisp wind can do the job just as efficiently, if not as dramatically. And even if you don't wind up being a medical emergency, you're almost certain to wind up cold, wet and uncomfortable.

It's so easy to stay warm and dry. You don't need elaborate gear, although elaborate gear can make the job easier if it's used with intelligence. Elaborate gear would have kept Ed and Charlie from being medical emergencies—maybe. A good night's sleep, a good breakfast, some knowledge of the countryside, a map, some notion of what the weather would be, spare gloves and socks, and something to munch on would have kept them out of trouble, even if their clothing was primitive, their physical conditioning nil, and their knowledge of body management nonexistent. They would have been uncomfortable, but they would have gained some valuable knowledge in the process. As it turned out, they did so many things wrong that it would be nearly impossible for them to sort it all out.

* * * * * * * * * * *

I'm no superman. I'm not the Great White Hunter. I'm a skinny forty-seven year old grandfather with gray hair and bad knees. I'm in decent shape, but cold weather can take a heavy toll on my scrawny frame. Although I'm outside a lot, I make my living indoors, like most people do. But I manage to stay reasonably comfortable in the outback because I've learned, through making a lot of mistakes, what to do and what to take with me.

I treasure my leisure time. I love my work, but right down there at the bottom line, I still work to buy leisure. We all do. And it seems to me to be monstrously foolish to waste that hard-bought leisure time being cold and wet and uncomfortable.

Let's do something about it.

Chapter 1

How Cold Affects You

—a

Most of us are pretty casual about getting cold in the summertime. Yeah, it happens. A sudden shower, a brisk breeze, and you're uncomfortably chilly. Fortunately, you usually bounce back. You put on a jacket, drink a cup of coffee—you know. No problem. Except for the discomfort, of course, which does louse up your pleasure of being outdoors. It's tough to concentrate on watching a size 16 dry fly bobbing down the AuSable when you're uncomfortably chilly.

But it's even harder to drop the post on a scope on the shoulder of a good buck on a 10° F morning when your teeth are chattering. You're not going to stop them from chattering by just slipping on a jacket for a few minutes. That's the whole problem in a nutshell. What's merely uncomfortable in summer can be debilitating and potentially dangerous in winter. And winter's when a lot of us are outside.

It doesn't have to be brutally cold, either. Ice fishing may be the coldest pursuit known to man that can be called "pleasure"—but ice fishing isn't what we read about in the papers or see on television when there's a story about some outdoorsmen suffering from "exposure". It's usually hunting.

Why? Well, to begin with, it's generally chilly to cold in hunting season. What's more important, though, is that hunting is an active sport. You're either walking constantly, or you've walked hard to get somewhere and then you've stopped. You've blown some energy, and you've worked up a sweat. In scientific terms, wet clothes — even damp clothes — are better conductors of heat than dry clothes. You cool off quicker. What happens next is the difference between discomfort and a helicopter evacuation.

You're a heat engine. You may be God's gift to the ladies and a good wing shot to boot, but you're still a heat engine, and you function pretty happily at about 98.6° F. The fuel you burn is food, and in cold weather, you'll burn a lot of it just keeping the machinery running. In fact, you'll burn off more than half again as much fuel in winter as you do in summer. Some of this is unavoidable. I don't care if you're swathed with goose down a foot thick, you still have to inhale cold air, warm it, saturate it with water vapor, and exhale it. This accounts for 18% of your heat loss, even if you're sleeping. Just saturating that cold, dry air with moisture takes up 9%. Evaporation of perspiration—not the kind that occurs from hard work, the kind that occurs simply because you're alive—takes up another 18%. Depending on the outside temperature, that's a minimum of 36% of your heat going somewhere else, and you can't do a damn thing about it unless you stop breathing.

What's left you can control. You control it by clothing and shelter, and by food. What happens when you can't control heat loss? You probably already know from experience. Scientifically, the process is complex. It can happen quickly; so listen up.

Within certain narrow limits, nothing much happens. You feel chilly around the edges. That's all. At about 95° F body temperature, you shiver. This is an involuntary reaction, an autonomic isometric contraction, if you will, to get things moving again—to force circulation, and to trigger a dumping of sugars stored in the liver. Below 95° F, the shivering becomes uncontrollable.

This is your last warning! The onset of uncontrollable shivering is your body's last effort to generate heat from within. If it can't, and you can't (or won't) provide either some means of stopping the loss of heat or providing heat from an external source, the situation deteriorates rapidly.

Write that down somewhere. Don't forget it. *If shivering doesn't warm you up, you cannot be warmed up without external sources of heat.* And if you can't manage to come up with some external sources of heat, you can die very quickly. Hey, I don't want to scare you. It's just that I'd like to meet you on a trout stream in the Upper Peninsula on a crisp May morning when we're both in our eighties, so you can tell me about some book of mine you read way back when that saved your buddy's life once.

Let's see what happens if shivering doesn't do it. Somebody's life may hang on your ability to know. If shivering works, the shiverer will probably complain loudly about how his fingers and toes burn. Fine. His extremities were well below 95° F, because his body had throttled down blood flow to them in an effort to keep the vital organs happy. This doesn't mean that everything is fine and dandy. Something caused him to get that cold in the first place. Whatever it is hasn't gone away. Chances are, though, that the emergency has passed. A dry undershirt and a couple of cups of hot soup or sugared tea or coffee will probably do the trick.

But if the shivering hasn't kicked in that stored glycogen in the liver, or there wasn't any left, the body shuts down blood flow even more. Remember, your body will sacrifice the extremities to save the core. Fingers and toes aren't nearly as important as heart, lungs and liver. And while the autonomic functions of your body will never completely cut off blood flow to your brain, it'll be cut back far enough that you won't be able to function rationally, if you can function at all. The extremities become numb; the victim's speech is heavy and slurred, almost like he's very, very drunk. In a sense, he is. Lack of oxygen to the brain is the culprit in both cases. He may mutter about feeling warmer. Don't believe him. He's dying unless you do something!

By this time, his blood pressure and pulse have dropped appreciably, and the combination of diminished blood flow to the brain and reduced dissolved oxygen in the blood have rendered him essentially helpless.

At this point, the downhill slide accelerates. The autonomic systems that have throttled down the blood flow to the extremities break down, and the already cool blood returns to the very chilled extremities to be cooled some more. The victim becomes comatose, and at a core (rectal) temperature of of 75°-80° F, he dies. Again, this process accelerates with tremendous speed at about 90° F body temperature. There is no predictable time frame in which that final, fatal drop will happen. You'd better be ready to do something, and do it fast!

But what? If you catch the whole thing early enough, like at the onset of shivering, the remedy can be simple. A dry undershirt, a cup of tea. A dry hat and mittens. Food is always useful. But it's a safe bet that the temporary chill was caused by damp clothing and aggravated by either dehydration or lack of readily available food for the body to use. Remove the cause, and everything will be fine. You've cut down on heat loss by taking off a wet undershirt and putting on a dry one. You've added a little heat, and a modicum of quickly available energy, with a cup of hot, sugared tea. And you've added some fuel to the shiverer's tank in the form of a peanut butter and jelly sandwich.

The process — remove the cause of cooling and add heat — is the same for the person who's passed beyond the shivering stage. But there's one major difference. This person's reserves are so low that simply removing wet clothing, and pouring some hot tea down him, won't bring him back. You start there, but you must do more. In order of priority, first reduce heat loss. Get the victim out of damp clothing and into dry clothing. If he's pretty well out of it, place him on the ground on all the clothing you can find to insulate him. Cut pine boughs if you must. (This is no time to think about damaging the forests.) Do what you need to do to keep him from losing more heat. If you have canteens, warm water in a fire, pour it in the canteens, wrap them in mittens or a shirt, and place them in the armpits, in the neck near the carotid artery, on the chest, and on the belly. If you can build a good fire close to him, do that too. If he's alert enough to swallow, hot beverages will help. Booze won't. Neither will a cigarette.

If you're out with a party, somebody should go for help. This is a genuine medical emergency, and it can be greatly complicated by diabetes or heart problems. It's nothing to fool around with.

If the victim recovers by himself, without being evacuated, the first thing he'll want to do when he gets back to civilization will be to jump into a hot bath or shower. Don't let him. Too rapid a rewarming, which will cause the return of massive amounts of still chilled blood from the extremities, can create a coronary incident that could be immediately fatal. Once he's past the danger stage, rewarm slowly. That goes for you too. Don't come into the house from a cold day hunting bunnies and hop into a hot shower. Wait until you feel pretty comfortable.

The medical term for this traumatic heat loss that we've been talking about is hypothermia. I didn't mention it right off the bat, because it's a current buzz word. "Oh, yeah. I know all about that stuff. I'll just skip ahead and find something else." That's how I react to the word. So if I tricked you a little bit, I apologize. But not too much.

Something else that's important to keep in mind about hypothermia: it isn't limited to winter. In fact, I'd wager that there are a lot more hypothermia victims in spring, summer and fall than in winter, although it's obvious that very cold weather can certainly bring it about easily. But cold alone won't make it happen, in most cases. It takes a combination — of cold, of wind, and of rain-soaked or sweat-soaked clothing. Given that combination, you can die on a fishing trip in 55° F weather. Or on an early fall deer hunt. We'll kick this around more later, when we talk about insulation and raingear. For now, let's look at that other medical problem that we associate with hypothermia and cold weather—frostbite.

In a sense, hypothermia and frostbite are closely related. They're both helped along by fatigue, lack of food, dampness, dehydration, and a lack of awareness that something is happening. The hypothermia victim, because his blood flow has been cut back in the extremities, is a ready-made prey for frostbite.

There's no mystery about frostbite. It's a burn, in essence, and is treated as such. It occurs when flesh is exposed to a combination of cold, wind and moisture, or it occurs when your circulation is diminished. Wet gloves and tight boots in cold weather will do it every time.

There's a difference between frost nip, which is really incipient frostbite, and the real thing. We've all had ears, nose, fingers and toes nipped a bit on brutally cold days. And except for an unpleasantly long-lasting tingle when you thaw out, no damage is done. The real harm comes when you're tired, down on food, dehydrated, and not thinking as clearly as you should be. That's when you don't notice the warning that frost nip gives you. Thereafter, true frostbite sets in.

Frostbitten feet don't feel cold. They're just numb. The water in the flesh has frozen, blood and oxygen are excluded, the nerve endings go to sleep, and your feet turn white, stiff, and very, very cold.

How can you keep frost nip from turning to frostbite? Move around if your feet are cold. Change your socks if they're damp. If your hands are cold, put on dry mittens, or put your hands under your arms. Hold a warm hand over your cheek, nose or ear. Don't go hungry, and don't go thirsty. The latter's not always easy to manage. You may have to carry a vacuum bottle of water in a pack, if you're in an area where water isn't available. Or you may have to melt snow for what the Alaska bush trappers used to call a "mug-up". Yeah. It's a pain in the butt. But not nearly as painful as losing three fingers.

Back when I was a kid, running a muskrat line through a swamp along the Mohawk River, I went out one morning early without the extra pair of mittens I usually carried. I wore mittens under the long rubber gauntlets that some folks still use for water sets, but it was only a matter of time before I reached in above the top of the gauntlet and got my left hand thoroughly soaked. Well, the ethics of the situation leave little choice. You don't walk away from a trapline that's only half checked.

To make a long story short, by the time I got home, my left hand was stiff, and my fingers and thumb stiffer. By some stroke of luck, nobody rubbed the hand with snow; neither did they plunge it into warm water. It thawed out very slowly, hurt like hell for a day, turned several lovely colors, and finally healed. My left thumb still suffers when it's nippy out, and it suffers promptly and in anything but silence. It's annoying—but it's a great early warning system! This

never would have happened if I'd remembered the extra mittens.

How do you treat frostbite in the field? Mild frostbite is readily treated by gradual thawing of the affected part. Don't rub or massage the part, please! There are millions of sharp little ice crystals in that frozen flesh that cut like so many knives. The best way to rewarm a frostbitten hand or foot is to place it against warm skin. If it's a hand, you can use your own skin. If it's a foot, it almost always has to be somebody else's skin. If there's a measure of real regard between people, it's the willingness to have somebody's frostbitten foot planted onto their warm belly. Laugh now. But if you have to do it, you'll do it. So will your friends. You'll know the treatment is working when the frostbitten victim starts to yell.

Any time you rewarm a frostbitten part of a body, get the hell out of the woods as fast as you can. That part is very vulnerable to further frostbite. Don't even attempt to rewarm severe, deep frostbite. Even if you managed to, assume that the victim is traumatized with deep third-degree burns and flesh that can be injured severely by a touch. Unless you're equipped to make a warm, comfortable shelter, and can medically evacuate the victim as soon as possible, and can maintain a sterile environment for the affected part, you're far better off to get out as fast as you can and head for medical assistance immediately. You run a risk of further damage from frostbite if you evacuate without treatment, but it's not as serious a risk as half-baked treatment.

Hospitals that see a lot of frostbite generally rewarm the affected part in a 105° F water bath. This isn't a treatment for the amateur in the field.

Most of the time, you can be outdoors all your life and never see any of this. A little cold? Yeah. Damn cold? Sometimes. Damp and wet? Sure; of course. A little frost nip? Who hasn't had that. We've all flirted around the edges of hypothermia and frostbite. It's not pleasant. Nothing can louse up a good day of fishing like a sudden rain when you're a mile from the car and don't have a rain jacket. So let's look at how to keep warm and keep dry in the field. That way, we won't even have to flirt with problems like hypothermia. We can simply have fun — and that's what we're out there for.

Chapter 2

Insulation:
What Keeps You Warm

You know, every time I talk to a group of outdoors people about staying warm and dry in the outback, there's always somebody who asks a question like, "All this jazz is fine, but why don't you just tell us what you wear?"

It would sure simplify my life if I could. Sit down, type up a list, and take the money and run. Neat. Unfortunately it doesn't work that way. I'm not you. My physiology, my body's response to heat and cold and rain and hunger and dehydration are similar to yours, but maybe not out there at the critical point that makes the difference between being alert and cozy when the buck jumps and being a congealed blot of protoplasm. The critical point makes the difference. If I'm happier in five degrees more heat than you are, I'll be better able to concentrate on fishing in a real scorcher. If your cold tolerance is better than mine, you'll get more bunnies on a chilly fall day.

What I need to keep warm and comfortable, therefore, may be a bit more or a bit less than you need on the same day. That nagging, niggling "bit" makes the difference. Better to know how insulation works, so you can figure out what works for you, than get a canned list from me.

Before we get down to the nuts and bolts about insulation, though, let's keep one thing firmly in mind. No clothing, in whatever amount you can imagine, will ever *produce* heat. All it can do is preserve heat that you're producing. If your body isn't cranking out enough to keep your body temperature at normal, or close to it, you'll be cold. Conversely, you can be buck naked and still be very overheated if your body's thermostat isn't working.

Don't get me wrong. You can get warm by putting on more clothes, or changing out of wet or damp clothes into something dry. Plain old common sense tells you that. But unless your body is cranking out the heat, those clothes won't do the job. You'll have to eat, drink, rest—maybe even start a fire to get your system rolling again, so you'll be producing heat for your clothing to conserve.

There are several ways we lose heat. Some of them we can't

control, like the heat loss that comes from warming and saturating the cold air we breathe. We can control other areas of heat loss with proper insulation and good judgement.

Conductive heat loss is both the simplest and most difficult to control. You lose heat by conduction when you touch something that's colder than you are. The plastic seat cover on my pick-up truck is a classic example. So is a wrench, or a shotgun barrel. But most of us don't go around grabbing cold objects barehanded in the dead of winter—or even on a pleasantly chilly day. But there's one thing you can't ignore. The earth. Chances are, you'll either be walking or sitting or some combination of both. Between your feet and your fanny, you can lose a lot of heat.

It's always amazed me that many hunters don't have the sense of Scouts when it comes to conductive heat loss via the cold fanny route. The Girl Scout has her little indoor project, called a "sit-upon", which back in my wife's day was an oilcloth-covered pillow. Primitive, but effective. And here's the Hero Hunter, wrapped in three hundred bucks worth of clothing, and carrying the finest in contemporary firearms, freezing his ass off sitting on a cold stump. Or worse yet, a cold rock.

Of late I've seen a lot more hunters using some sort of insulated pad to sit on, but it still seems to me that most of the guys out there haven't gotten the message yet. Perhaps they think that it's less than manly to be warm. Hey, I used to take a lot of kidding about my little foam pad and the little stove in a small daypack and all those other luxuries I'd tote on a hunt. But I don't remember anybody ever refusing a hot cup of coffee at 4 o'clock in the afternoon on a cold, windy day in November!

The other conductive heat loss problem is through your bootsoles. That's a very special problem that we'll kick around in a chapter all by itself.

The second common mode of heat loss is by radiation. Radiant heat loss happens when the outer layer of insulation is warmer than the air outside. Bare skin on a cold day is an obvious radiant heat loss. In general, though, if your insulation is adequately thick for what you're doing and the weather you're doing it in, radiant heat loss is not significant.

The real bugaboo is convective heat loss, in which cool air in motion whisks heat away from our warm bodies. This is the toughest to control, because so many factors come to bear on it. And there's never a static solution to convective heat loss, either. Bundle up, shut off all openings that the wind can claw at, and you'll soak your insulation with sweat. Wet clothing sets up a combination heat loss situation—conduction and convection—and you're losing heat at a dangerous rate. Dress too lightly, and the wind penetrates your clothing and whisks the heat away into the south forty.

Can you win? Probably not, if you just depend on your insulation. You have to manage the situation a little. The simplest, most effective set of rules for managing your body came from a French workman and bicycle nut, who formulated them back around the turn of the century. His name was Paul de Vivie, and he wrote, often and well, for the bicycling press under the pen name of Velocio. Here they are, and they're as good now as they were then —

1. Eat before you're hungry.
2. Drink before you're thirsty.
3. Peel off before you're sweaty.
4. Put back on before you're chilly.
5. Rest before you're tired.
6. Avoid tobacco or alcohol while riding.
7. Don't ride just to prove you can do it.

Old de Vivie knew what he was talking about. And he was talking to trained athletes. You may think bicycling is for kids, but the professional road racer is probably the best conditioned athlete in the world—or, at least, right up there with the cross-country ski racer. What works for them will work even better for you.

But let's find out what this insulation is that we're supposed to manage. There's no mystery about it, advertising claims to the contrary notwithstanding. Insulation is a thickness of *something* around you that provides for a certain thickness of undisturbed air. In the strictest sense, a vacuum bottle is the ultimate insulation. There's no air between the double walls to move. You can't conduct heat from one molecule to another, because there aren't any (actually there are so few) molecules to bump into one another. Convective losses can't take place either. We naturally can't wear a vacuum bottle. We have to settle for something less than theoretically perfect because we still have to be mobile. This means that our insulation must be light and flexible. The problem with light, flexible insulation is that wind penetrates it easily. So we encase our insulation in fabric, or wear a fabric that's insulation in and of itself to keep the wind from zinging on through it. If the fabric covering is too sleazy, we lose too much heat through convection. If it's too dense, we sweat, and we find the garment stiff and difficult to move in. Again—you can't win. But you can break even.

Probably the commonest insulation the outdoorsman wears is

wool. Shirts, pants, jackets, sweaters, socks, mittens—you name it. Lately, we've found some reasons—many of them good ones—to abandon wool in favor of some synthetics. But before we make a mad dash to the research chemist's latest product, let's see what over two hundred breeds of sheep have given us.

A fiber of wool is pretty complex. There's an inner cluster of cells surrounded by an overlapping sheath that looks like nothing so much as the scales of a fish. The chemical composition is keratin, a long-chain molecule of protein formed by eighteen amino acids. These little devils are coiled in intricate ways. The result is the typical crimp in wool that's the key to its resiliency and its insulating power.

Further, wool is mostly air, dead air. In little pieces, as it were. And little pieces of dead air are at least as critical to a garment's insulating properties as thickness alone. True, an inch of down and an inch of newspapers may present the same theoretical thickness and insulating value, but the amount of dead air that is trapped along the thousands of feet of surface of the plumules is terribly difficult to dislodge. This "boundary layer" of still, warm air hangs in there when the going gets tough. Wool's the same way. The dead air trapped in the fibers and along the fibers is tenacious. It also keeps you insulated.

Think of it this way. Water flows around a big rock in the middle of a stream. But if I break that rock up into a lot of little rocks, I can create a dam that slows the river appreciably, because there is a lot more surface area for the water to work around, and a lot more immovable boundary films of water against those little pieces of rock. In the same way, if heat escaping from your body has to work through millions and millions of tiny fibers. It's simply tougher for the heat to leave.

Wool works pretty well in damp and wet conditions, too. To begin with, your perspiration passes through it easily, so your underclothing doesn't get as clammy as it might with other materials. Yet wool can wick up moisture, either from sweat or from rain, and not feel too sodden.

Everything isn't a bed of roses, though. Any material that permits perspiration to blow out through to the outside also lets winds to roar on through to the inside. That's the old "there's no free lunch" principle. And while wool that's absorbed up to 30% of its weight in water doesn't feel unpleasantly wet, you've still set up a marvelous blanket over you that will transfer heat to the outside world very efficiently. In other words, you'll be fairly comfortable while you get cold.

In short, for all its virtues, wool is best used as an intermediate layer of insulation in severe or wet environments. There it works. Elsewhere, it may or may not. And even if it does, you pay a heavy penalty in weight.

For really keeping warm, there's still no substitute for down. It has drawbacks, but it's superbly light, very compressible, and has a pleasant feel when you're wearing it. It fits, if you know what I mean. It goes where you go. In the jargon of the garment trade, it has a "good hand".

Down is, of course, a natural product, and is subject to considerable variation. Most of it comes from the Orient; some of the best comes from Northern Europe. And it's a by-product of raising ducks and geese for market. This fact, oddly enough, has made prime Northern European down particularly costly. Why? Family size has gone down, particularly in Poland, over the last twenty years. A smaller family doesn't need as big a goose for dinner. Smaller, less mature birds have fewer down plumules, and less well developed ones to boot. Hence, prime down is scarce and costly.

When down, either duck or goose (prime or run-of-the-mill) arrives here, it's a mess. It comes in big bales that usually leak, and it's incredibly cruddy. Ducks and geese aren't the most fastidious members of the animal kingdom. It gets steam cleaned in huge rotating drums, which helps to clean things up a bit, and then it's sanitized and sterilized. Next, the dry down is blown into something that looks like a fractionating column at an oil refinery, and works almost the same way. The small plumules are sucked out of the tower at the top, the bigger ones in the middle, the feathers further on down, and the dirt and the crud and the huge feathers sink to the bottom. The down is then blended to conform to several grades, which are defined by fill power (one ounce of down will fill a certain volume, usually expressed in cubic inches) and by ratio of down plumules to feathers. California, Colorado and New York are particularly fussy about what constitutes "down", and if a product that purports to be goose down is either made or sold in any of these states, it has to meet stringent specifications. I can remember when I ran an outfitting shop. The New York State "feather merchant" came in regularly, cut open a few bags and jackets, and took samples of the down back to a lab for analysis. It was a pain in the butt. I'd have to return the bags to the manufacturers for credit, and some of my inventory would be unavailable for sale for a while, but in the long run, it was worth it. Particularly when the "feather merchant" would pull a bunch of junk bags or jackets off the local schlock house's shelves because they were falsely labeled. I have to admit that it didn't hurt my business either.

The bottom line with down is that you get what you pay for, for the most part. If you're buying fashion, all bets are off. But if you're buying a functional down jacket, the price is a realistic representation of the quality. There's a difference between down that lofts up to fill 450 cubic inches per ounce and down that lofts up to fill 550 cubic inches per ounce. The difference is resilience, longevity, consistency, uniformity, and warmth per unit weight. You pay for the difference. You also pay for the difference in needlework. The outfit using low-grade down typically sews it in a perfunctory manner, and uses fabric that costs less because it has fewer threads per inch. It may look good to an untrained eye. But it isn't. We'll look into the differences later, when we start talking about what results when you start sewing up insulation into clothing.

But—before we leave down, let me make two statements that fly in the face of a lot of advertising. To begin with, the measure of good down is not whether it's from a duck or a goose. The measure is its fill power. Period. Generally, duck down won't have the fill power of goose down, but I've seen some duck down that lofted to over 600 cubic inches an ounce, and that ain't too shabby. Finally, the difference between white down and grey down is color. Period.

If you think that down can be a bucket of worms to investigate, you haven't seen anything until you've looked into the synthetic insulations. You can hardly tell the players even with a scorecard!

Let's go back some years to my youth. Unless you could find an old G.I. down and feather bag in a surplus store, or had the bucks to buy an Eddie Bauer bag, or had the persistence to buy a bag from Thomas Black's in Scotland, you lived with a cotton poplin bag containing reprocessed rags or kapok. Remember them? They had pheasants or deer printed on the soft cotton liners, and they had little stand-up tentlike hoods that funneled the rain right down into your neck? They weighed twelve pounds and they rolled up into something that looked like a carpet. You kept warm in your house, maybe, if it wasn't a cold night.

I fished the Quebec and Ontario bush for two summers with one of those suckers, and damn near froze to death every night that I didn't wear all my clothes to bed. (I did other things wrong, too. But we won't go into that right now. I'll display my foolishness later.)

Then one day, out of the blue, came this miracle fiber from DuPont. Dacron! Fluffy white stuff that looked like a bundle of 6x tippet material. By today's standards, Dacron wasn't much. But by the standards of the time, it was sensational — reasonably light, could be dried in the field, and was fairly compressible so you could actually carry a sleeping bag inside a pack — if it was a BIG pack. And it was cheap. Furthermore, the whiz kids with their retorts and test tubes kept improving it. Others got into the act. As of this moment, there are several synthetic insulations that are almost as light as down per unit of fill power, are anti-allergenic, can be dried in the field, compress nearly as well as down, and are reasonably inexpensive.

We could discuss the merits of the various synthetic insulations from now until hell froze over, and while we'd both learn a lot, it'd be a long, strange trip. What makes more sense, assuming that all the better-known brand name synthetic insulations work well, is to look at a few ways of thinking.

Insulation can be effectively measured in terms of loft, or thickness, of a garment or a sleeping bag. It can also be measured indirectly by the number and the size of the tiny, tiny fibers that make up the insulation. Remember the big rock in the river and all the little rocks? Superfine fibers trap more undisturbed air next to their surface than do fat fibers.

So, as would make sense, we have some of the heavy hitters in the insulation trade pursuing thick, poofy insulations that work and feel much like down, and some pursuing boundary-layer insulations that act like wool.

All synthetic insulation is made in a similar fashion. The fibers are extruded from multiple showerhead nozzles much like a spider extrudes its web. In fact, the nozzles are called "spinnerets". The material, usually polyester but perhaps polypropylene, may come out as a microfiber or a somewhat thicker fiber. It may be hollow, or it may be solid. It may be spun out into a felted batting, or it may be chopped into short lengths, in which case it's called "chopped staple". It may even be woven into what looks like synthetic fur, called fiberpile. Each of these materials has a wide range of applications for which they're well suited. Alas, some are better than the others for certain things. And that's a function of how they work in a garment rather than a function of their insulation value *per se*. Again, we'll talk about that when we talk about garments.

With all this talk about insulation, I reckon it's about time to talk about how much is enough. Fortunately, I don't have to go through a shuck and jive routine here. I can crib from the Army Quartermaster's Corps, an indispensible source of information on how people interact with the realities of the physical world. This graph shows you

Insulation for Various Activity Levels

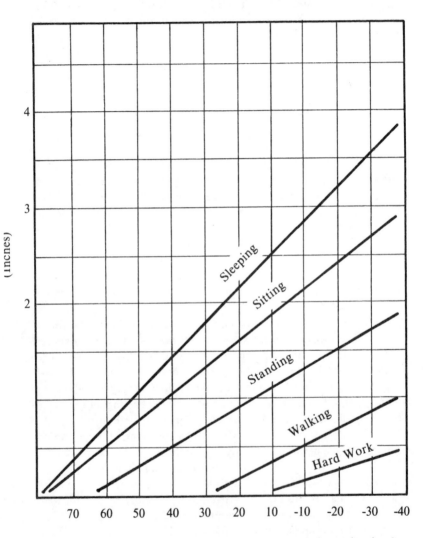

Temperature (° F) at which a heat steady state can be maintained.

the amount of insulation needed for various activities at various temperatures. It makes some assumptions, though. It assumes that the insulation is sufficiently dry, and that the activities are carried out in still air. It's also assumed that the participants are healthy and well-fed. In other words, this graph demonstrates the possible rather than what really happens out in the field. Still, it's a useful guide, particularly in those areas dealing with the amount of insulation required when you're active. I can tell you for fifty pages that you don't need much on you on a still, cold day if you're moving. This ties it down in numbers.

Another bit of hard data regarding insulation may be of interest to you as well. The British, as would befit a nation that invented dry fly fishing and mountaineering for sport, enjoy long-distance walking competitions. They're usually held in damp, rainy, chilly weather—as if there was much of a choice! The walker's attire is light. Typically, it's shorts, a fishnet shirt, a light wool sweater and a nylon windshell. Deaths from hypothermia have occurred on these walks, at temperatures well above freezing, but with high winds present and the inevitable rain. After the deaths of several competitors in one competition, a British physiologist, L. Pugh, measured the insulation value of the walker's garb when dry, and then again when wet. The measurement is expressed in clothing units, or *clo,* and one clo is the equivalent of a conventional business suit. The walker's clothing measured 1.8 clo when dry, and 0.18 when wet *in a windless environment.* In other words, the wet clothing had only a tenth of the insulating value of the dry clothing, even under optimum conditions. Pugh, with typical British thoroughness, next measured the insulating value of that same wet clothing if a waterproof jacket was put on over it. The value was 1.0 clo, or over five times that of the wet clothes alone. Less, to be sure, than the clothing measured when dry, but enough warmer to be merely unpleasant rather than deadly.

File Pugh's experiment in the back of your mind. You'll see how it can be applied later.

Chapter 3

Vapor Barriers:
Steam Heat In The Field

Mountaineers are cagy folks. Some might add "crazy" to that as well, but I've had a lot of fun scrambling up mountains, some steep, some less than steep. I've learned a lot from it, as well as had a lot of fun. What I've learned is that when you're carrying all your worldy needs in one small pack, you'd better be damn sure that each item in that backpack is worth its weight in function. If it doesn't buy you anything, leave it at home. And if it doesn't work, get something that does.

Telling you it's cold in wintertime isn't news. Telling you that big mountain climbers, working at high altitudes, in thin air, and in bitter weather, frequently manage to stay quite comfortable with what they can carry on their backs, might be.

The big mountain guys pioneered the use of all kinds of clothing that you now see, much modified, in every supermarket in America on a chilly day. Down parkas, down vests, hooded mountaineering windshells—you name it. It strikes me as strange that the makers of clothing for the field sports have taken until now to borrow some of these very functional ideas from the tops of the world. Stranger still is the fact that millions of hunters and fishermen have never come near a shop that sells backpacking and mountaineering gear. Yeah, the gear is expensive. So is a graphite fly rod or a free-spool casting reel.

Be that as it may, the high elevation folks have been playing around with a new concept of insulation lately, and from what I've heard and from what I've tried, it works. It's called *vapor barrier insulation,* which is based on a couple of simple, easily proven assumptions.

The first assumption is that wet insulation can kill you, because it sets up an evaporative cooling cycle that can rob heat from your almost as fast as immersion in bitterly cold water. Our redoubtable Britisher, L. Pugh, already showed us that. And our own experiences have shown it, too. Get your clothing sweaty and it's damned chilly.

The second assumption is that we sweat to keep our bodies cool when we're working hard. No argument there; that's how the system works. There's a sneaky little extra here, though. Our bodies sense when to sweat, and how much, by the amount of moisture on the skin already.

This means that we can cheat our bodies a bit by maintaining a constant low level of skin moisture, and reduce overall perspiration. Thus our clothing are kept drier. How to do it? Wear something next to your skin, or in close proximity to your skin, that is impermeable to water vapor, and put your insulation over it. Simple. And it works. You do have to monitor it, however. You still don't want to get soaked because it's uncomfortable. When you stop, you'll feel cold. Remember, for comfort you'll be wearing something light, like a fishnet shirt or a polypropylene undershirt, under that impermeable jacket. That'll be wet—but the down or synthetic stuff that really keeps you warm won't be.

Some climbers go the vapor barrier one step better and use a heavy windshell or even an impermeable rainshell over their insulation layer as well. This way, the insulation is kept dry from both perspiration and rain and snow.

The vapor barrier idea works. And yes, it feels funny. It takes some getting used to. It also means that if you stop, as you might on a deer stand, that you should probably change out your undershirt. This idea is foreign to most hunters, who prefer to take little, if anything, with them. Remember, I carry a small pack. There's room for an undershirt in it. And dry socks. And that lovely little stove!

Probably the optimum uses for the vapor barrier principle have little to do with major items of clothing. Let's face it. Most of us don't put out the effort in the field that you do at 23,475 feet on a vertical ice face. And thank God for that small favor. Where we can derive the benefits of vapor barrier insulation is in the hard to insulate places like feet and hands.

Plastic bags next to your skin feel funny. Maybe even worse than funny. However, a plastic bag over a thin pair of socks, with a couple of pairs of wool socks over them, is a sure way to keep your socks dry. Which means warm. And a cheap rubber glove, or the super-thin plastic gloves that hairdressers use, with gloves or mittens over them, and a shell mitten over the whole array, is truly warm hand insurance.

How do I know hairdressers use thin plastic gloves? My outfitting shop was next to a hairdresser's, and I used to buy plastic gloves from the guy for my customers. And that's the name of that tune, smart guy!

Another useful area for the vapor barrier is to extend the range of your sleeping bag. Most of us can't—or choose not to—afford a summer sleeping bag, a three season sleeping bag, and a winter sleeping bag for late season deer hunting or summer trips in northern Minnesota. Here's where the vapor barrier really shines. Take your summer bag, add a vapor barrier liner, and you've added probably 10° to 15° F to the low end of the bag's comfort range. Now put that same bag, plus vapor barrier liner, into an outer shell, be it waterproof or water-repellent, and you've bought another 5° F or so. Presto! Your 30° F sleeping bag has just become a 15° F bag, and if you put on a pair of long johns — *dry* long johns — when you sack out, it may even be a 10° F bag.

If you can't find a vapor barrier lining, check with your local backpacking shop and buy some lightweight (2.2 oz/yd) coated nylon, and sew it into an envelope that fits inside your sleeping bag. Do the same as an envelope for outside the bag. You can almost dispense with a tent.

Some cautionary notes on vapor barriers, though. Above 45° to 50° F, you'll sweat like a pig in a vapor barrier. Unless you plan for cold weather in the offing, and that 50° F night was an accident, don't bother with the vapor barrier. If you know that it's going to get colder, it may be worth a clammy night with the liner in place just to keep the bag dry against the upcoming cold snap.

So—vapor barriers work. They buy a lot of warmth for little expense and even less weight. And they buy you a lot of comfort in the field, too. And that, my friends, is the real bottom line.

Chapter 4

Raingear

Rain is a fact of life. Granted, it usually presages lousy hunting, deer being smarter than men in this instance, and it may or may not bring on lousy fishing. As for other outdoor activities like canoeing and trapping, better you shouldn't ask. But the weekend or short vacation might be all the time you have to get outdoors for awhile.

Raingear gives you a choice. You can get wet from the outside in from the rain. You can get wet from the inside out, from sweat. Or you can do a little of each. Not your basic clean-cut choice.

New fabrics and construction methods have greatly broadened the uses of raingear. But whatever the material, and however highly it's touted, you can still be miserable if you haven't picked the right garment and the right material for what you're doing.

Let me give you an example. I like to hike. We were scrambling our way up a trailless peak in New York's Adirondacks on a drizzly, chilly day. I was wearing a poncho and Molly was wearing a rain jacket and rain pants. Well, when you're scrabbling your way through six-foot balsam growing six inches apart on centers, you're going to hang up a lot. That poncho caught on every branch in the universe—and they were all there to catch on! Molly slid through easily, of course. And when we got to the bald rock summit, the wind picked up. I mean, we're talking *wind,* friend. Sixty miles an hour or so. That poncho was like a big sail. I could see myself being whisked off the summit and sent flying down a very steep two thousand foot high ridge. Or, more accurately, I couldn't see. The poncho had blown up around my face, and wouldn't unwrap. It was cold, it was embarrassing, and it could have been very dangerous. That poncho was an admirable piece of raingear. But not in that situation. Not by a long shot.

On the other hand, I've spent many comfortable afternoons in a downpour, fishing little meadow streams with that poncho. Works fine for that.

Does this mean that you should consider several pieces of raingear? 'Fraid so. What works in one situation may be totally inappropriate in another situation.

Let's look at the types of raingear available, and see what they can do for you.

PONCHOS are favored by a lot of people. They're easy to get on and off, even over a pack. They're loose enough that they ventilate well. The design—a square of waterproofed fabric with a hood in the center—is easily made, and thus relatively inexpensive. And they can do double duty as ground-cloth, as tent, even as camouflage blind.

However, rain running off a poncho will soak your legs and feet unless you're wearing something waterproof. In a brisk wind they're a horror. And I'd rather be wet than wear one in a canoe, especially in a moving river.

PARKAS are what we think about mostly when raingear is mentioned. And this figures, because they come in an almost bewildering variety of styles, fabrics and construction methods. What makes a parka a parka? The full-length zipper down the front. It's both a blessing and a curse. The zipper—which may be a two-way zipper system that opens from the top down and the bottom up—allows ventilation in a drizzle, or even when it isn't raining at all. This helps you stay dry from the inside out, and adds a real degree of flexibility to the garment. After all, if you can ventilate it, it's useful as a windbreaker, too.

But that full-zip front can backfire, too. The seams running down the front—the seams used to stitch the zipper in place—have been known from time to time to spring leaks, and even those official-looking storm flaps that cover the zipper are frequently little more than funnels for carefully directing the rain to the zipper.

Furthermore, parkas are frequently designed as multipurpose garments with lots of doodads. Pockets all over the place, hoods that tuck into cunning little openings in the collar—you name it. But every seam is a potential leak. Every pocket is a potential impromptu, and unwelcome, canteen. And a hood that isn't being used in the rain because you prefer a hat is little better than a portable goldfish bowl without the goldfish.

The *ANORAK* is a parka stripped to the buff with a short zipper. You have to pull it on over your head, which isn't bad in the outback, but is a distinct nuisance when you're trying to look suave and debonair for some young lady's delectation.

The anorak doesn't ventilate as well because of the short zipper. It lacks the pockets of the parka, although it may have one kangaroo-style pocket in front. Also, it's harder to find, because most people prefer the versatility of the parka. However, it has fewer seams to leak and is generally a more functional piece of raingear.

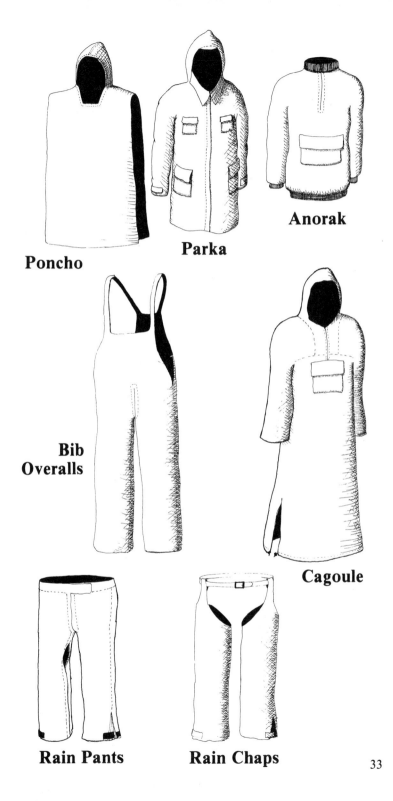

Poncho

Parka

Anorak

Bib Overalls

Cagoule

Rain Pants

Rain Chaps

33

The *CAGOULE* is an anorak that reaches to below your knees —unless you're a power forward for the San Antonio Spurs. It's long enough that you can sit down and draw your knees up inside, snug up the bottom drawstring, and fend off both the elements and the black flies at once. It's closed on the sides so it doesn't get whipped around in a wind. Unfortunately it doesn't ventilate very well.

The cagoule was born as a high-elevation mountaineering garment. For some climber forced to sit out a night on a ledge two thousand feet above nothing, the cagoule was a portable tent that you wore. They work well in terms of protection, but they're a bit clumsy to walk around in because they limit the length of your stride. And like ponchos, cagoules will ride up your legs as you walk, allowing rainwater to run down your shins and into your boots.

There's one hidden "plus" about a cagoule. It's a garment designed and built for very severe duty.

RAIN PANTS keep your trousers dry. A parka won't. A poncho won't. An anorak won't. Even a cagoule won't. Water running off your raingear will soak your trousers, and if the wind is blowing, you can get very chilly indeed, particularly if you're wearing cotton pants. Cotton is a comfortable material, but it loses its air spaces when it's wet, and it hangs next to your skin like a sheet of water. In cold weather, or wet windy weather, this can mean Hypothermia City. So, if you like cotton pants for field wear in spring, summer and fall, rain pants are of great importance to you.

The problem with most rain pants is that they don't ventilate well. It's tough to ventilate warm air from around your waist, even if you wear loose rain pants and suspenders, because your waist—and well below your waist—is covered by a parka or a poncho or an anorak. The solution is to find a pair of rainpants that ventilate at the groin, which is the area of greatest perspiration after your armpits.

Most rain pants are cut full enough, and have tabs, snaps or zippers at the cuff, to allow you to get them on and off without taking off your boots. You can check this out at your outfitter's shop easily enough. It isn't any fun to have to take your boots off to put your rainpants on in the middle of a very heavy downpour.

And while you're checking out the pants, make sure they're long enough to cover your boot tops while you walk. Otherwise, your pants will be dry and your boots will be full of water. There's nothing more unpleasant than boots full of water, believe me!

RAIN CHAPS are just what the name implies. In essence, they're pantlegs with straps on them that loop around your belt. They're very light and easy to carry in the smallest of packs, and they certainly ventilate well around the groin because there isn't anything there. A simple, elegant solution, as the engineers would say. Of course this can cause a problem when you sit down on a wet, mossy log—unless your parka or whatever is long enough to cover your butt. In fact, if your parka is short, and the wind's whipping up a bit, you just may have two little rivers running down your legs under the chaps. This unpleasant experience is a close second to slogging around with your boots full of water.

BIB OVERALLS provide the maximum protection, extending up over the chest, under the arms, and up the back. This naturally means another layer of clothing over what you're normally wearing. If you're walking up a steep hill, for example, you'll get very hot and sweaty indeed.

For some activities, notably canoeing and fishing, I find them just about perfect. Hey, when you're nine miles offshore in Lake Huron trolling for salmon, you're exposed to whatever's coming down. There's no place to hide. You need all the protection you can get!

And don't forget a *HAT*. Marvelous apparel, hats, in winter and summer. I know that your super miracle fabric parka has a hood on it. The hood doesn't leak, and it's comfortable. Fine. That's a bonus. But your scalp and the nape of your neck comprise fifteen percent of your body's heat regulatory mechanism, and under extreme conditions, nearly *thirty* percent! On a warm day, or when you're working hard, you need to keep some of that elaborate network of veins, arteries and capillaries uncovered to dissipate heat, just like to have to keep that network covered when you're cold. It isn't easy to ventilate with just a hood. A hat works better because it doesn't cover the nape of your neck and shield your throat. The combination of a hood and a hat gives you all sorts of options.

I find that hoods are frequently an annoyance, even in cold weather. Hoods impair my peripheral vision, and more importantly, impair my hearing.

The design of any rain garment is important. So is the way it's put together. But no garment can be any better than the basic fabric from which it's made. That fabric ultimately determines the water-proofness, the durability, and that intangible "feel" that's so important in the field.

The least expensive rainwear fabric is *VINYL*. It will certainly keep you dry; there's no doubt of that. It gets brittle quickly with age and in cold weather, and is generally made up in very rudimentary garments. Handy items like pockets, zippers, waist drawstrings and such may be found on a vinyl rainsuit, but they tear off easily.

However, if all you want is a cheap waterproof parka and pants suit to keep the rain off you while you're sitting in a boat and fishing, vinyl will do the job for you. For anything more complex, or for long-term use, forget it.

The standard material for raingear has been, for some years, *COATED NYLON,* which is simply a woven nylon fabric to which one or more layers of coating have been applied.

The commonest coating is *POLYURETHANE.* It's light, flexible, reasonably durable, and it works. If you store it wet for extended periods, or keep it in the trunk in the dead of summer, you could have some peeling of the coating.

NEOPRENE is a synthetic rubber coating that's used frequently on work rainwear, like telephone linesman's gear. It's heavy, in general, because it's usually applied to a heavy, rugged fabric. In the lighter weight fabrics, neoprene is extremely durable and is usually built into garments with vulcanized seams which don't leak. Breathability? Nil. Less than nil, probably. And the typical neoprene garment isn't built with many bells and whistles.

ACRYLONITRILE is another synthetic rubber compound used frequently on heavy-duty raingear. It's expensive and twice the weight of a similar thickness of polyurethane, so it's not too great if you have to carry it in a pack. It's tough to a fault, though, and if you really like standing by your downriggers in a rain squall on Lake Superior in early May, it's appropriate rainwear.

If vinyl raingear is known for its cheapness and its brittleness, *POLYVINYL CHLORIDE* (PVC, or "vinyl coated") raingear is noted for its strength. Of all the coatings, PVC is the only one that actually increases the strength of the fabric. PVC raingear is the standard raingear of the commercial fisherman, and if it can survive autumn on the North Sea or off the New England coast, it's obviously quality stuff.

And heavy stuff, too. A rainsuit (parka and bib overalls) in the classic heavy-duty commercial PVC rainwear weighs about what a scope-sighted big game rifle weighs. In other words, it's not exactly the gear you want to put in a pack and tote around the countryside for a day or two.

Coated fabrics work. They keep the rain out. But just as they don't let moisture in, they also don't let it out either. Perspiration can't pass through the coated fabric. Furthermore, in cool, humid weather—or in cool weather when you've been working hard enough to break into a sweat—moisture will condense inside the raingear.

This isn't much of a problem if you're sitting in a canoe, fishing.

36

But if you're walking up a long hill with a pack on your back, it'll be a problem. The only way to overcome that problem is to pay attention to what you're wearing under your raingear — unless you want to solve the condensation problem by liberal applications of rectangular dollars. Materials exist that will keep you dry and "breathe" at the same time. And they all have something in common—users swear by them or at them. There seems to be little middle ground.

By far the best known of the "breathable, waterproof" materials is *Gore-Tex,* and following it is its clone, *Klimate. Gore-Tex* and *Klimate* are not fabrics in and of themselves. They're very thin, microporous films of polytetrafluorethane, or PTFE, and they're bonded by microdot adhesives to fabric. Don't let the fancy label of PTFE throw you; it's Teflon, the same stuff that keeps fry pans from sticking, except in the case of *Gore-Tex* and *Klimate,* it's expanded into what looks like a tiny screen under a microscope.

How does it work? Simple. All you need is a screen small enough to keep water droplets out while letting water vapor pass through in the other direction. Water molecules are small, like 2.76×10^{-8} centimeters in diameter. But water molecules are cozy things. They like to cluster up with their buddies. They like to form drops of water rather than stay as individual molecules. These drops are bigger than the pores of the expanded PTFE grid. They can't get through—but water vapor can.

Fine. In theory. But theory doesn't always translate into practice. While PTFE laminates can transmit water vapor almost as fast as plain old cotton, the garment itself will be warm. In the case of the heavy-duty PTFE laminates, in which the PTFE layer is bonded to a 3.5 ounce/yard nylon exterior shell and a nylon tricot liner, the garment is probably as warm as a heavy woolen sweater. And that's enough to make you sweat, regardless of how much water vapor the fabric can transmit. Further, the cut and the finishing details of a garment mean as much, assuming the integrity of the fabric, as the fabric itself.

Unsealed or poorly-sealed seams will leak. A poorly designed hood will let rain in underneath—and let it trickle down your chest. Pockets are great catchalls for water, as are zippers. In other words, the material may be fine, but somebody botched the design or the execution.

Does PTFE work? Yes, again with the *caveat* about the seams and the design. It transmits water vapor well; it resists rain. True, some of the early PTFE material was subject to leakage if contaminated by dirt or body oils. I had one particularly fine parka that went to hell in two years from that problem. The newer stuff, the "second generation" PTFE, seems to have overcome this problem, but I'd still pay close attention to the marker's instructions regarding washing. But this goes for more than PTFE laminates. You can louse up any garment by improper care.

Gore-Tex and *Klimate* aren't the only materials billed as waterproof and breathable, though. Probably the first such material was introduced by Peter Storm, and was called *"Bukflex"*, a polyurethane film bonded to a knitted Dacron polyester liner. The material has been modified in detail if not in substance over the years, and is now called *"No Sweat"*. It's very waterproof, with taped seams and a simple garment design, and it does transmit some water vapor. It doesn't "breathe" as well as the PTFE laminates, but it's eminently durable. It breathes well enough to keep you dry from the inside out, unless you're really working up a sweat.

And then there's *Storm Shed,* a treated blend of tightly-woven polyester-cotton that's almost a throwback to the old days of cotton raingarments. *Cotton* raingarments? Sure. Waxed and oiled cotton was commonly used as raingear way back when. You can still find motorcycling waterproofs made of very heavy cotton. Well, *Storm Shed* isn't cotton, and it isn't coated with heavy, inflexible gunk. In fact, it feels just like conventional 65% Dacron polyester and 35% cotton. It's breathable, and it meets the Quartermaster Corps standard of 25 PSI water entry pressure. It's a compromise, though. It isn't perfectly waterproof, because it's virtually impossible to seal the seams. It breathes well, but not, at least on paper, as well as *Gore-Tex* and *Klimate*. It's better in a drizzle than the coated fabrics, because it breathes better and keeps you from getting soaked from the inside out. But there's one thing it does better than any of its more exotic nylon rivals: it is relatively quiet going through the pucker-brush. Unless you're hunting, this is no big deal. But if you're hunting, and there's a chance of a light snow or a drizzle while you're afield, *Storm Shed* may just be the material you'd prefer.

You can talk forever about the benefits of each material, and you won't settle a thing. The bottom line is that the fabric alone doesn't make the rain garment; the design does. And design isn't an either-or proposition. It's a series of compromises. Ponchos ventilate well, but they're hell in a wind. A parka with a lot of pockets is handy, but each seam is an open invitation to water unless it's been heat-sealed by the maker—in which case, it's apt to cost a fair chunk of money. What can you do? First, figure out what you want the garment to do. Yeah, I know. You want it to do everything. You want to be dry on Lake

Huron in a late spring downpour, and you'd like it to be yellow so the Coast Guard can spot you if things get bad. But you'd like it to be very breathable for bunnies in the fall, and preferably in fall camo with a blaze orange patch on it. On the other hand, it should be breathable, warm and very resistant to the encroachment of wet snow when you're out on the back hill in January calling fox. Of course, it should be white, too. You can't have everything. Figure out in your own mind where you need the most protection, and what bells and whistles you need, and you'll be halfway there.

For example, a hood is great if you're backpacking or fishing from a boat. It's worthless if you're actively hunting, because you need your ears. They're at least as important as your eyes. Pockets are useful if you want to go down to the river and fish without taking a mountain of gear. A little *Plano* box stuffed in one pocket will do the job. As you won't be too active, you can choose a material that's very sturdy and waterproof. But that same garment may be a poor choice for canoeing, at least if you're an active paddler.

Okay. Your choice of garment pretty much depends on what you plan to do while you're wearing it. Really, that's no news; you didn't have to buy a book to find that out. The real problem comes when you need raingear for four very dissimilar pastimes and have money enough for one jacket! But that's no news either. If I had my way, I'd own ten fly rods. I don't have my way. I own three, and one of them, an old South Bend split bamboo job my father bought for me when I was eleven doesn't get used too often, although it's still pretty lively.

At any rate, it if you're not loaded with dollars that you're just itching to spend on a complete wardrobe of outdoor rags, it behooves you to look closely at what you buy, and get good value for your money.

How do you tell good value? It isn't always easy. With high-ticket stuff, you can almost always assume that what you're getting is well made. With lower priced garments, you can't always tell. Take good old, simple coated nylon, for example. The fabric can range from 80 threads per inch to over 120 threads per inch. The coating can be minimal, or it can be double-coated. The garment can be cut full enough to fit over your clothing without cutting off circulation around the armpits, or it can be cut so skimpily that you'll pop a seam if you inhale. The jacket can be sewn together with one quick pass of a needle and thread, or it can be sewn neatly, with ten to twelve stitches per inch. The seams can be puckered or neatly done. The unfinished side of the seam can be whipped to keep the fabric from unraveling, or it can be taped, or the loose edges can be tucked and stitched down—or you can have a nice raw edge that will unravel in time. Generally, the better stuff will cost more, but not always.

One of the real problems is that a lot of schlock clothing manufacturers discovered a long time ago that hunters and fishermen were uncritical buyers of clothing. The motto seems to be, "If it's in red, orange or camo, they'll buy it without looking." Consequently, I've seen a lot of junk in hook and bullet shops that wouldn't ever get into a good work clothing store or backpacking shop. And what really frosts me is that the price for the junk is the same—or more! Fortunately, some very good clothing manufacturers have entered the field sports market. And a lot of general backpacking and mountaineering clothing is beautifully applicable to field and stream use. Some of the gear is well-nigh perfect. Not cheap—but it does what it has to do. And some of the very best comes in sizes up to XXXL!

So, don't limit your clothing hunt to just your friendly local gun shop. Look around. Order out catalogs. Read. And look at the garment in the shop! Here's what to look for:

Start with seams. And remember the three rules of seams.

1. *As any seam can leak, the fewer seams there are in the first place, the better off you'll be.*

2. *Pockets are little more than seams stuck out in the rain. The fewer seams stuck out in the rain where they trap water, the better.*

3. *Seams should either be factory-sealed or capable of being sealed with a liquid seam sealer.* While fancy seams like overlocked or flat-felled seams won't stretch out and open up, and are easier to seal, they'll still leak, because water will follow the needle hole.

However, you can seal some seams all day, and they'll leak if they're in the wrong place. The seam that attaches the hood of a parka, poncho, cagoule or anorak to the garment body is susceptible, because rain can blow up under it, and a wet snow can just hang there all day. The same with the seam over the hood. It's vulnerable to wind. Occasionally, you'll find a parka with a one-piece hood. It's not common, because it leaves a lot of scrap on the cutting room floor.

Most raingear has seams on each shoulder; one in front, the other in back. This may be cut like a yoke, an unfancy Western cut in other words, or raglan cut. Water can find these seams, and if they're sloppily done, they may be tough to seal. Some manufacturers make the whole upper body of their rain garments in one piece, and seam them at the waist, which is usually less vulnerable to rain. This is a lavish way to cut a jacket. Bring money.

Underarm seams and seams along the side of the garment are usually well-protected from rain, but this doesn't mean that they should be badly done. The mark of a good garment is one in which every seam is well-executed, whether or not it's truly critical. You can't help but feel that whoever sewed it cared about what they were doing. No manufacturer is perfect all the time, but a good garment house works to do it right, inspects rigorously, and stands behind their warranty. You pay for this—but then you pay for the fact that there aren't any Monday morning fly reels made at Hardy's either.

Then there's the zipper. Parkas have them; anoraks have them. Zippers leak. While a lot of light-duty raingear doesn't have flaps over the zippers, the heavy-duty stuff should. Flaps aren't a cure-all. My favorite piece of heavy-duty raingear, a PVC coated nylon parka made for the North Sea fishing trade and for offshore yachtsmen, has a full-length *Velcro* strip to seal over the zipper, and all the seams are electronically welded. That zipper is dry, dry, dry, believe me. You can stand out in the cockpit of a salmon fishing rig on Lake Huron in a downpour that'd do credit to a fire hose, and you won't get Drop One of water through that zipper.

Nothing's perfect, though. The hood is badly cut. I wear a hat over it!

Storm flaps with snap fasteners on them look neat, and all that jazz, but a good wind-driven rain will find those openings as unerringly as a good quarterback will find the seams in a zone defense. For heavy-duty gear, I like that full-length *Velcro* strip. Sure, you'll still have seams to seal, flap or no, but it's a lot easier to keep the water out of those seams than out of a zipper.

Most of the PTFE raingear on the market today has factory-sealed seams, and a lot of the heavy-duty gear made for offshore sailing and commercial fishing is factory-sealed as well. Yet, factory sealing isn't a cure-all. Check the seams carefully. Vulcanized, heat-sealed and electronically welded seams are usually trouble-free, unless there's a loose edge or a wrinkle at some point where rain running down the outside of the seam could pop in and say "Howdy". And if the seams have been sealed at the factory with liquid seam sealant, it won't hurt a bit to do it again. Frequently only the critical seams have been sealed, and a lining sewn into the garment. This means that you can't get inside to seal the seams where they should be sealed for best results; nevertheless, a carefully done outside seal will work just about as well. I'm a belt and suspenders man myself. I seal the seams on both sides, and I do each seam twice. It doesn't look pretty on the outside, but I'm not out there to impress anybody with my sartorial elegance. I'm there to stay warm enough and dry enough to hit that brace of high flyers when they come screaming in.

Hoods are useless for the most part. Not because a good hood can't turn a lot of rain, but because there are so few good hoods around. A properly designed hood must fit the face snugly, yet it must be cut in such a way that you can turn your head from side to side without pulling. Further, the hood should seal under your chin, not over it, so that rain dripping off your face won't run down inside your parka. Finally, the hood should do all these things—even if you're wearing it over a thick woolen cap or Balaclava. Frankly, a good hood will do most of these things, but not all, and a bad hood won't do any of them. A great hood? I've run across three in my lifetime.

This isn't so much a knock at the manufacturers as it is an indication that hoods are difficult to cut. What fits you perfectly may fit me badly, and vice versa. I have a large head—7¾ is about it—and a long neck that's surprisingly thick. Otherwise, I'm a stick figure. If you cut a hood for me, it wouldn't do very well for somebody more normally proportioned. But this wouldn't bother me so much if there were a lot of hoods that fitted more conventionally assembled people. There aren't. The solution? Wear a hat that will turn some of the rain that the hood can't reach. Be thankful that the hood protects the nape of your neck, and don't worry about it.

Pockets? Pockets are the enemy as far as staying dry, but pockets are so handy that it's almost impossible to get a garment without them. Sometimes, you'll find inner pockets sewn to the lining of a parka, so that the stitching doesn't penetrate the outer shell, and these are worth their weight if for nothing more than car keys and a place to stash your pipe and tobacco. Cargo pockets, those big jobs hanging on the outside of a parka, can be great repositories for lunch, sunglasses, and all the myriad things we all clutter up our lives with. So you might as well reconcile yourself to the fact that your parka will have pockets. I've found that the kind of pocket that seals with a double roll of fabric, and fastens down with *Velcro,* just like a dry bag for canoeing, is the dryest pocket around. Just be sure to seal the seams!

Some of the super parkas have other useful features like underarm zippers. There are three places where it's practical and efficient to ventilate a parka when you're walking. The first, and simplest, is to throw back the hood and unzip the zipper, but this won't work in a rain. The next obvious area is around your groin. If you don't cinch up the drawstring, and if you're not wearing a pack, this is fine. But in a wind-driven rain, or with a pack on, every hatch is battened down. The next obvious place is to ventilate under the armpits, and some of the most refined garments made have underarm zippers. They work. It's a great idea for ventilation. It's less great for rain protection, though. It isn't easy to seal the seams on an underarm zipper, and because you can't have a lot of bulk there, these zippers are rarely, if ever, covered with a storm flap.

All of the gadgets and doodads, however useful, aren't worth a hoot if the gear doesn't fit. Don't try on raingear over a T-shirt. Try it on over what you'd be normally wearing. If there's a choice between too loose and too tight, opt for the loose. The garment will ventilate better, and you'll still retain freedom of movement. It's tough to swing on a mallard when you're in a straight jacket. If you can raise your hands up over your head without having the jacket ride up over an inch or so, and without having your wrists exposed halfway up the forearm, you're close. And if you can touch your elbows together in front of you, and still not feel restricted across the back, then you've found something that fits. Sure, your buddies will tease you about the sack you're wearing, but when the rain comes beating down, and you're warm, dry and mobile, and they're not, they'll all be asking where you got that sack, who made it, and how much did it cost.

Fit, function, fabric—all these play a part in raingear. But no raingear will keep you dry all the time, and in all conditions. The best you can hope for is to be mostly dry most of the time. Why? Because, come Hell or high water, you're going to sweat, and even if no water leaks in from the outside, there will always be some water that you'll generate that wants out. In other words, what you wear under the raingear is as important, if not more important, then the raingear itself.

Whatever you wear underneath your raingear should be barely warm enough to keep you comfortable when you're moving. It's easy enough to put on something warm when you stop. Just don't bundle up for a long trek over the ridge to that secret trout pond, and get there with all your clothing soaked from sweat. You'll be plenty warm in summer with next to nothing on under your raingear, as long as you're moving. In fact, one of the virtues of the cagoule, that mountaineer's garment that looks like a high-tech granny dress, is that you can truck around even in public with it on, and somewhat less than the law allows on underneath it.

Okay. You wear as little as you can get away with under the raingear when you're moving. Or when you're just sitting there throwing a Little Cleo at a reluctant salmon. Make sure that what you wear underneath will provide some insulation when it's damp. Cotton is a bummer. Sure, it's comfortable, but it dries slowly, loses its air spaces when it gets wet, and can chill you to the bone even in balmy weather. Wool? Fine. Polypropylene? Great. Fiberpile? Probably too warm for summer use except around camp, but worth more than its weight in pure gold when you need it.

One more thing. Getting wet can be a hazard in the best of weather. Other times, it's nothing more than an inconvenience that you'll joke about over coffee the following week. But it's never pleasant. Even with the best raingear and the best body management, you can fall off a log crossing a stream, or slip when you're wading, or dump a boat. You're suddenly and unexpectedly wet. However a small pack with a change of clothing in it can brighten your day immeasurably. Spare clothing and a dry sleeping bag can salvage a weekend from chaos. These things may just save your life if push comes to shove, but don't think of them that way. Think of them as trip insurance. If Ed and Charley, our two sweaty, weary hunters in the introduction, had a small pack containing a change of underwear, a parka, socks, mittens and something to eat and drink, they would have had a fine day. So can you.

Chapter 5
Clothing

We all run across it. Here's an ad in the local newspaper that features down jackets at the ridiculously low price of $39.95. Your friendly local outfitter sells his down jackets, that look pretty much like the sale item at the local schlock house, for $82.50. Hey! Somebody's ripping you off! Or are they? You can't always tell unless you know what to look for.

There are no secrets in the rag trade. Any good garment house can tell you to within a nickel what it costs them (and their competitors) to cut a particular garment. If they couldn't, they wouldn't be in business for long. This means that there really aren't any "steals" in clothing. Or in anything else, for that matter. Unless you're lucky enough to catch a dealer selling out because he went broke, or running a sale because he overbought warm gear in a warm, rainy winter, nobody's giving anything away. Nor should they. The economics of the system are inexorable. Sure, your outfitter may have paid $60 for a jacket he'll sell to you for $100, but he's had to buy 96 garments to get the size and color you want, and he's paid his employees, and paid a lease on his shop, and a few other things. In the end, he clears five bucks on that sale. Nobody gets rich being an outfitter, unless he's turning a helluva lot of five dollar net sales in the course of a day.

I've been there. I know. A lot of my time back in the '60's and early '70's was spent explaining to quite a few folks that they weren't getting ripped off, and that I was entitled to make a small, if pleasant living, for my labors.

So much for that. Knowing that the outfitter isn't hosing you may be nice, but it doesn't tell you how to figure out what's good and what's schlock. Let's start from the inside out with rags to see what works, and why.

SOCKS

Socks? Big deal!
Very big deal, in fact. Socks keep you warm in cold weather; they

cushion your feet as you walk; they wick perspiration away, to keep you from swimming in your own sweat. Socks are often sorely neglected.

As far as I'm concerned, the name of the game is wool, preferably in a blend of wool with some nylon or *Helanca* for wear resistance and stretchability. There are all sorts of strange socks with funny weaves that wick moisture away and all that jazz. The wool blend holds up well. It cushions your feet nicely, transmits some moisture (call that "sweat") away from your feet, and it's warm. You can't ask for more. This type of sock, often called a ragg wool sock, is generally available now. You can depend on your local backpacking shop to have them in stock all year round, rather than just in winter.

I like to wear them over a very thin wool liner sock, which I much prefer to the synthetic liners. They feel better to me. Perhaps not for you, so try both. Why the liner? Simple. The outer sock will rub against the inner sock instead of against your foot. Rubbing creates heat, which creates blisters.

What about socks to wear under boots? You can get high-topped ragg wool socks in good old traditional gray or tan, or if you want something noisier, like red for hunting season, you can get that too. What are they called? Lots of things, but mostly they're called knicker socks. Cross-country skiers wear them.

Here's a case in point. There are lots of clothing items that will do the job of keeping you warm and dry that you may have to find outside of the normal outlets that cater to "sportsmen", whatever they may be. I've been kicking around the backcountry for years, and I haven't figured out what a "sportsman" is. But I have long since figured out that the folks behind the counter at the local backpacking shop, who regularly roam around the mountains when the temperature is somewhere on the dark side of -25° F, know a lot about keeping warm. I might not go to them for recommendations on handloads for my old '06, but I'm not going to ask my local handloader, who hibernates when the weather gets below freezing, for information on winter clothes, either. Make use of expertise whenever and wherever you can find it. Get quality whenever you can afford it; because it's cheaper in the long run.

Back when I was younger and dumber, I bought high-topped boot socks for hunting and trapping by the gross. My feet were always cold in those cotton monstrosities, and they wore out at the toes and heels quickly. They were cheap, though. About half the price, or less, than a good pair of wool socks. The price ratio still holds—but I have some wool socks that I've used very regularly for over five years. And I'm lucky enough that I don't have to dress for success every day. I wear my wool socks and casual clothing even for business. Those socks see a lot of wear and tear. They've not only lasted, they've kept me warm and dry.

UNDERWEAR

In summer, I wear a pair of cotton Jockey shorts and a net T-shirt, but even in summer I carry a pair of lightweight poly-propylene long johns—tops and bottoms. Long johns in summer? Why not? The top is great under under rainwear because the polypro transmits moisture through it, and dries almost instantly in a little sun and a light breeze. And sometimes at night, if it's a bit chilly, or my old bones are a bit tired from a hard day in the field, those lightweight long johns feel just great around the campfire. About the only time I wear cotton in the field is when I'm canoe racing in hot weather, where I can actually get a considerable cooling effect from that sweat-soaked shirt that feels like it's growing from my skin.

In winter, I'll stick with the lightweight poly, or substitute a heavy poly undershirt with a couple of buttons in the front for ventilation. Sometimes, if I'm planning to be relatively sedentary for long periods of time in cold weather, I'll wear a lightweight wool long john set (85% wool, 15% synthetic). Sometimes, in bitter weather where there's a good possibility of winds, I wear a pair of poly undershorts that have a nylon panel to keep the chilly breezes away from a very sensitive and hard to insulate part of my anatomy. Greatest thing since sliced bread, believe me! They're marketed under lots of different names, but most of the trade refers to them generically as "peter heaters".

What don't I wear? Cotton, or cotton blends. I don't care if there's a wool layer over the cotton, that cotton will get wet from sweat, and chill you in a hurry. I concede, though, that the cotton blends are very comfortable when I'm reading or writing or tying bass bugs. But that's it. Except for those cotton undershorts in summer, cotton has no place in your wardrobe for the backcountry.

Underwear is pretty simply sewn. There isn't much to check out except the obvious. Are the seams sewn well, so the garment won't unravel? Fine. Is the fit acceptable? Generally, I prefer wool blends to be a bit loose, and poly a bit more form-fitting. I have no deep, dark, scientific reason for this; it just seems to work better for me. If it fits, fine. As to styles, the wool blend tops I prefer have a couple of buttons down the front, to enable me to ventilate myself when I need to. So do my heavy polypropylene shirts. My lightweight poly tops are crew necked, although I have one turtleneck that's a real favorite of mine for cross-country skiing when I'm wearing lightweight clothing and really want to run on my skis.

PANTS

In summer, wear what's comfortable. I like the cotton-polyester blends, and I generally avoid jeans. They're impossible to dry when they get wet—and they will get wet! Unless you've worn them for years, jeans are usually too stiff for comfortable movement. In cold weather, wool's the name of the game.

As with raingear, less is more. Pockets are fine, and should have flaps that can be closed with a button or Velcro. Too many pockets are a nuisance. More seams to snag, more places to rummage through when you want your pipe lighter, more places to put things in that rightly belong in a small pack. A multiplicity of pockets looks great in the shop, but have you ever tried walking somewhere with eight pounds of junk in your pants pockets? And have you ever tried sitting down with your pants pockets so laden? That's what packs are for. Yeah. I know. "Real outdoorsmen" don't carry packs. But the guys who go out in deer season and find those "real outdoorsmen" when they get lost, with no spare food or clothing, wear packs.

Don't size your pants for fashion. Keep them fairly loose and comfortable, and don't let the legs hang down so far over your boots that you could catch a heel in them. Further, when you go to your outfitter's for raingear, or even a pair of windpants — simple uncoated nylon pajama pants that will turn a lot of snow in winter —wear the pants you'll be wearing in the field, and try the raingear on over them. That way, you'll know whether or not you have a good fit. Anything else is guesswork.

The folks that do pleasant little hikes in the mountains, like climbing near-vertical ice walls at 24,500 feet in a blizzard, have adopted some very untraditional approaches to clothing in the effort to simply stay alive. Pants, in the normal sense, don't make it. They're simply too constricting and not warm enough. These folks have adopted a material that looks like fake fleece. It's made of polypropylene and is called, generically, fiberpile. You've probably seen it in jackets; the pants are rather more esoteric. And they're not really pants. They're more like sweatpants. They're very comfortable, and permit a full range of motion. They're very warm if you wear them under a shell garment that keeps the wind from penetrating them, and they dry very quickly because the material itself absorbs essentially no water. They're funny looking, but with a pair of poly long johns under them, and *Gore-Tex* or *Klimate* all-weather pants over them, you're *warm*. Moreover, this combination breathes very well indeed, and stays dry even when you're walking hard. In the past, this gear was virtually unknown except to climbers, winter hikers, and whitewater paddlers. Now it's more widely distributed. Furthermore, *Gore-Tex* and *Klimate* garments are now available in colors that are more suitable for field sports, including both tan and green camouflage. You're thinking that poly, pile and PTFE might just make it in a duck blind? You're thinking right.

SHIRTS

In cold or rainy weather I generally use a pile jacket with a full-length zipper as a shirt. I didn't in the past, and I don't always now. The polyester blends are great for summer and early fall outings, and you can get simply made, rugged ones at any work clothing store.

Wool shirts? Why not. They do the job, they feel right, and they look right. I'm partial to the double-yoked shirts that Woolrich makes, but these are fairly heavy for most uses. A medium-weight, tightly-woven wool shirt, with button-down pockets and a long enough shirttail to cover you comfortably when it isn't tucked in is a most useful garment.

A hint: the classic Norwegian net undershirt, or a more modern equivalent, is just about perfect for summer wear under a light shirt. It'll keep you cool, and it won't mat down like a wet blanket in even the hottest weather. On a cool day in early fall, the net undershirt under a wool shirt is very pleasant. If it gets chilly, or if the wind comes up, a rainshell will turn most of the wind, and you'll still stay dry if you remember to unzip the jacket.

There shouldn't be any great mysteries in selecting a shirt. If you're like me, you wear what you have, and patch it if it gets torn. Again, though, look for comfort in a fit, rather than style. Take the time to check out how securely the buttons are attached; resew them at home if you need to. It's a good idea to check those old shirts before your next trip as well.

INSULATED OUTERWEAR

Along with raingear, insulated outerwear is that part of the backcountry roamer's attire that's most frequently misunderstood, and most frequently wrapped up in a sacred mantle of Tradition. I appreciate some elements of Tradition. However, I prefer a graphite fly rod to a split bamboo rod. I loathe wooden gunwales on canoes almost as much as I loathe flat bottoms and keels on canoes. I find the traditional lever action "thutty-thutty" to be a poor substitute for the contemporary bolt action rifle. And if you catch me using a canvas tent, you'll know that I've taken leave of my senses. By the same token, it'll be a hot, rainy thirty-first of February before you see me decked out for deer season in a heavy red and black checked woolen jacket and pants, with a blaze orange plastic bib and cap. There are easier ways to keep warm. And the key to keeping warm is the insulated parka.

When we talked about insulation earlier, we didn't get into what happens when the insulation is sewn into an outer garment. Now it's time to look closely at the garment itself, because insulation alone is just the beginning. I've seen prime down sewn beautifully into totally non-functional garments, and I've seen relatively low-cost synthetic insulation sewn cleanly into very functional outerwear—and I've seen everything in between.

Insulation isn't a simple thing. There's insulation that entraps a thickness of dead air, like down. There's insulation intended to trap a less thick block of air along the lengths of tiny microfibers, like *Thinsulate* or *Sontique*. And there are synthetic space-filler insulations that come in bats, and some that come in chopped staple. Each one needs to be handled differently in a garment. And each one offers something that the others don't.

Let's start with down. It's the lightest of all known insulation materials per unit thickness. It clumps badly when it's wet, and dries slowly, if at all, in the field. It loses thickness quickly when it gets damp. It likes to meander all over the place; so it has to be sewn into small, discrete tubes to keep it where it'll do you the most good. Some care is required in washing, and it conforms so beautifully to your body that wearing it is a joy. Be careful about wearing it waterfowling from a boat. If you fall overboard, your goose'll be cooked!

Most down garments that you'll find in shops are of two basic types: quilted (sewn through), or quilted with an overshell. You may run across an occasional expedition parka that's sewn like a sleeping bag, in box-section tubes. These are rare, very costly, and of little use in the field unless you plan to hunt iceworms on Denali Pass in mid-January.

The sewn-through jacket is a simple unit. You know that you'll lose some warmth where the inner and outer shells of the garment are sewn together to form the tubes, because you know that you can't fit any down in between those stitchlines. And you know that the front halves of the garment will be sewn to the back of the jacket with a sewn-through seam, in all probability. Some high-quality jackets aren't sewn this way, and it's easy to spot them. There'll be a definite free-floating thickness of insulation around those side seams. By the same token, the sleeves of a good jacket will be attached to the body of the jacket in such a way that there's insulation over the top of the shoulder. This obviously requires more sophistication and time than simply cutting two sleeves, a back panel, and two front panels, stuffing the suckers, sewing them up, and then sewing them together. This is the kind of stuff you're apt to find on sale for $39.95 at Cheap Charlie's.

Okay. Barring the obvious junk, how can you tell whether Brand A is worth twelve bucks more than Brand B, assuming both are pretty decent to begin with?

First, shake the jacket a bit, and pat the down around in the tubes so they're all filled evenly. Hold both garments up to a strong light and see how much down is in the tubes. If a tube only looks half filled, if there's a lot of space above the down and below the stitchline, a lot of precious warmth will blow out of that jacket. If the tubes are well-filled, fine. There'll always be a little space there, but there shouldn't be much. Remember, the jacket you're looking at in the shop is dry. The down should be at maximum loft. If that tube is only half-filled now, think of what it'll look like after five days at hunting camp, after it's gotten damp, and been squashed and pummeled.

Next, check the general level of needlework in the jacket. Sloppy, irregular, crooked stitching and dangling threads are as acceptable as frayed leaders and bent shotgun barrels. Nobody who builds quality garments will accept sloppy needlework as a matter of course. Sure, even the best make a mistake. We're all human. But if most of the garments from one maker on the rack are sloppy, you can bet your last nickel that the stuff is junk.

If the jacket has an overshell, is the overshell made of either a densely-woven, tough fabric or a PTFE laminate? And if it's a PTFE laminate, are the seams sealed at the factory? They'd better be, because it's probably impossible to get inside that shell to seal them properly if they're not.

I'd advise against the PTFE-shell down jacket, and against a PTFE-shell synthetic jacket as well. They're fine parkas. They're warm; they shed water well; they breathe acceptably. But unless you have a very specific use in mind for one—say deer hunting—and will be using it a lot for that purpose, you get a lot more flexibility and adaptability for about the same money by buying a simpler insulated jacket, and using a separate shell garment as required. That way, you can use the shell parka to turn the rain and the wind in summer, too—which is difficult if your only PTFE garment is a heavy, insulated parka. On the other hand, if you have the bucks and the need, they're lovely coats to have.

Note, though, that I'm not advising against the insulated parka with a sturdy polyester/cotton blend outer shell. While I prefer the lighter, more stuffable, more comfortable ripstop nylon or nylon taffeta insulated parka, the heavier fabric is probably quieter in brush, and a lot more resistant to snagging. I wear a shell over my lightweight nylon down parka, but if you view this as a nuisance, or an unnecessary expense, by all means consider the parka with the heavy-duty outer shell. This outer shell, be it the actual "skin" of the jacket or an overshell that encloses a simple sewn-through parka, will inhibit the loft of the down a bit, but I doubt if it will cost you five degrees of warmth. You can make up for that by pulling your hat down over your ears!

The fit of a down jacket is as important as its construction. One of down's great virtues is its "hand"—its softness, its ability to move with you. Even under a heavy-duty mountaineering parka three inches thick, you can move almost as freely as if you were naked. But there's nothing free. This "hand" is bought at the expense of warmth if the jacket is too snug. That lovely, compressible down simply flattens out to next to no thickness across your back and shoulders if the garment is too snug. If you can touch your elbows together in front of you without feeling any pull across your shoulders, the jacket fits well. Check sleeve length, too. If you're using the coat for deer or bunny hunting, do you have enough sleeve length, and enough room under the arms to swing a gun without having the sleeves ride up your arm and restrict your movement? Try it and find out. You may feel like a damned fool swinging an imaginary shotgun in a store filled with people, but if that's the purpose for which you plan to use the coat, it had better fit properly. And console yourself with this. If you think you look funny with an imaginary shotgun, think about the dude who plans to wear the jacket for climbing vertical walls of ice. He's reaching around like a spider doing push-ups on a mirror in front of everybody. And over in the corner, a skier is boogeying down an imaginary mountain checking out the fit of a coat. Of course, you have to remember that in a nation where most people prefer to watch cliff diving at Acupulco on the tube rather than hoist their butts out of their chairs and *DO* something, anybody who goes outside for any purpose beside getting to the car is bound to be suspect.

A couple of other things to check, while you're at it. Look at the seams inside the jacket. Are they covered with a thin strip of material so they won't fray? It's called a "taped seam", and it's a neat touch. Another way to keep seams from fraying, and ultimately self-destructing, is to bind the seam with an overcast stitch. Either will work, although the taped seam is neater. A plain raw seam is prime evidence of schlock work. How do the cuffs fit? Can you snug the cuff down to keep out those chilly winds and still use your arms freely? Storm cuffs, those cozy knotted, elasticized jobs you'll find on lots of jackets, are comfortable and allow for a degree of flexibility, but they attract water like a magnet attracts iron filings. They're acceptable for field wear if—and it's a big "if"—they're tucked back under the protection of the outer shell of the garment. Otherwise they're useless if you really plan to keep warm and dry.

Some parkas come with integral hoods, others with snap-on hoods you can buy as an add-on feature. You know my opinion about hoods in general. They're of limited use even when they're good, and worse than useless when they're not. Check the fit of the hood carefully, and try to do the things you'll have to do when you're wearing it. If it works, fine. If not, look for another parka. The snap-on hoods are pretty much useless except for walking the dog or hanging around camp. They're generally far too skimpy in their face coverage to be really effective in the field.

In a sense, there's no difference in the way you look at any parka, be it down or synthetic, other than evaluating whether or not the insulation is sufficiently well controlled that it will keep you warm without leaking heat to the outside. Other than that, you're evaluating coats on how well they meet these three criteria: function, function and function. At risk of being repetitious, if it doesn't work for what you plan to use it for, it's useless. I own an expedition grade down parka. For years it was my constant companion on some severe mountaineering trips in the dead of winter. It's long, thick, the hood is superb, and at a whisker over three inches thick it's almost an ambulatory sleeping bag. I can think of no more useless a garment for deer hunting than that parka, though. And it's scarcely more useful for any other field sport except ice fishing. Out on a big, bitter, windswept frozen lake, though, that sucker's in its element! The only reason for an ice-fishing shanty when you're wearing that parka is to have a convenient place to put your lunch so the peanut butter and jelly sandwiches don't freeze.

The synthetic insulations, either of the space-filler type, like Du Pont's *Hollofil* or Celanese's *PolarGuard,* or the boundary-layer type, like 3M's *Thinsulate,* won't offer you the marvelous feel of down, or the extremely light weight, but they offer a few things that down doesn't. Probably their most prominent advantages are cost and the ability to be dried quickly if they get wet in the field. Cost is pretty much self-explanatory. But don't expect a dramatic difference in cost between a well-made down parka and an equally well-made synthetic. While down is a lot more expensive per pound, you rarely find more than twelve ounces of down in a parka, and the needlework requirements are very similar. You pay for materials in a parka; there's no doubt of that. The best always costs more than the worst. Sometimes a lot more, if you look at prices paid by garment makers for bolts of fabric. But the real cost difference is in assembly time—labor costs, in other words.

Your best outerwear may appear more simple and uncomplicated than some of the cheap stuff meant for drugstore cowboys and suburban leaf-rakers, but believe me, that simplicity is strictly simplicity of appearance. The patterning, and the resulting sewing, is more complex. The seams are complicated to sew. The zippers are set in with double-needle machines. The hoods may be cut with seven or eight pieces rather than two—and fit like it. The shoulder and arm insertions are done in long, precise curves to provide extra room, and they take longer to sew. All the raw edges are bound or taped. PTFE shells are sealed at the factory, and the machinery to do that sealing is costly and fussy to use. These are the differences that add up to far more than just the price of the raw materials used in the parka. And what you get as the ultimate user is fit, function and longevity. Sure, you pay for it — and save in the long run.

A little while ago I picked up a new fishing vest—a Columbia Henry's Fork model, if you're curious. I've coveted a Columbia vest for years, but it always seemed a lot of money to put out for a vest when I could get something that would work after a fashion for half as much. Well, in the twenty-odd years that I've salivated over the Columbia vest, I've gone through three lesser vests, and probably wound up spending twice what the Columbia would have cost me in the first place. None of the "bargain" vests really did the job! That's not economy. That's damned foolishness! Will I catch more fish because of that vest? Probably—because I'll feel better in it, and it can carry what I want where I want it carried. It frees my mind from the nitty-gritty and lets me think of fishing. That's what any good garment does—it doesn't interfere with what you're doing.

Back to the synthetics. You can generally assume that a good synthetic parka will overcome one possible deficiency in a down parka, that of continuous insulation. A quilted or sewn-through synthetic parka won't be as thick at the stitchlines as it is when the insulation is free to puff up, but there's still something more there than two lonely pieces of nylon or cotton/polyester blend standing between you and the cold, cruel world. Other than that, check out the synthetic parka like you'd check out the down parka. Will it do the job for you, and will it hold together when you use it? There's no mystery to that.

Sooner or later, if the synthetic parka is what you want, you'll have to choose between the space-fillers and the boundary layer insulations. My advice is to shop somewhere where both are stocked so you can get an honest evaluation of the differences. This is more important than you think. I work for a company that builds very high-quality canoes in fiberglass, *Kevlar*-reinforced fiberglass, vacuum-bagged *Kevlar,* and *Royalex.* I can give you a straight-forward, honest evaluation of all these materials, because we do them all. If all we did was mold boats in *Royalex,* I'd be busy feeding you that old line about glass boats shattering if you said "rock" in their presence. Same with your outfitter. If all he carries is *PolarGuard,* a very good space-filler insulation, he might be tempted to knock the other space fillers and really do a hatchet job on *Thinsulate*-insulated garments. If he carries several kinds of insulated parkas, he'll be more interested in fitting your needs than selling the only parka he has on the shelves.

Anybody who hangs around the trade as long as I have has heard horror stories dealing with every insulation material known to man, and probably some that aren't. "Hey, did you hear that so-and-so (a very reputable manufacturer) ran laundry tests on *Thinsulate* and it just fell apart? The rep says it's real junk." Or how about this one? "Did you hear that so-and-so (another very reputable house) only guarantees their *PolarGuard* stuff for a year? They did some life tests on it, and they said that it loses all its loft." Then there's this one. "Naah. All the down jacket people rip you off. The ones that didn't get caught using substandard down bought their way out of it. So-and-so? A buddy of mine told me that their stuff was the worst of the bunch, but they knew somebody. You know how it is."

No, I don't. I know of no insulation that's been marketed in my years in the trade that didn't work pretty much as represented. Sure, maybe some bozo who was cooking up a blend of goose liver sausage and rabbit tails to stuff into his own sleeping bags didn't quite make it, but the biggies—and synthetic insulation is the exclusive domain of the heavy hitters with millions and millions to spend on development—aren't playing games. Sure, the newest insulation on the block will send the old boys back to their labs to take it apart, and doubtless, they'll find something wrong with it. On the other hand, the new guys already found something wrong with the existing material, and walked into fill what they saw was a vacancy in the market. The bottom line is simply this: all the major contemporary synthetics work pretty much as advertised. They all feel a little different, and drape a little differently, and have to be sewn in a slightly different fashion. You'll find that they'll all keep you warm and dry if the garment they're made up in is well designed and well sewn.

What do I like? I like *PolarGuard* because it lends itself to very simple garment construction. Being a continuous filament fiberfill, it doesn't require as much quilting for stabilization, but this also means that seams are often fatter than they might be. I like *Hollofil II* and *Quallofil* also. They're chopped staple, which means that they need more stabilization, which increases needle time and labor costs, but they're both very compressible so you can stuff garments in a pack more easily. They have a feel that's as close to down as you can get. I like *Thinsulate* and its DuPont-engineered rival, *Sontique,* the boundary-layer insulations, because they can be sewn simply into garments that are very trim and free from bulk. They don't stuff quite as well in a pack, but you can't have everything.

Again, assume that the insulation will do the job, and get the garment that does what you want it to do and fits properly. You're not evaluating trout flies, where maybe only one will do the job on a given day on a certain section of river. You're evaluating clothing that hopefully will do a lot of jobs for you. It'll never do all of them. For years I've coveted a three-quarter length (almost knee-length) insulated parka of the sort that goose hunters use out in those cold goose pits in the upper plains states. Not for goose hunting, mind you, but for late fall drift fishing for steelhead. How nice to have a really warm butt for a change, if you know what I mean. You see, I'm one of those clowns who stands up in a canoe. There are times when the chilly winds get to me. But at the price those parkas go for, I can't justify buying one for that very limited purpose. Some day, maybe. When it's a choice between a frozen butt and steelies, I'll find the bucks to chase the steelies. And so will you—or you wouldn't have been reading this book in the first place. Hey, you can always make do with last year's suit. This is pleasure we're talking about, Jack!

There's another insulation I've played around the edges with in this book, because it really doesn't fit into any one category. That's fiberpile. And while it's an insulation, it's also a garment in and of itself. And yet, to be an insulator, fiberpile has to be a part of a system of insulation that begins with underwear, goes to a pile jacket, and is topped off, whenever you need wind and rain protection, with a PTFE shell parka.

I haven't used fiberpile long — about five years. In that time, it has grown to be the Great Indispensible of my wardrobe. By itself, it's comfortable in still air at very low temperatures, and it's still comfortable at 65° F on a January morning when you're camped at Rabbit Key in the Everglades. If I get it soaking wet, by design or by accident (yeah, I tip a canoe over now and then), I can wring it out and put it back on under a shell. It'll dry on my body and feel warm and furry. In fact, I'm wearing a pile jacket right now, as I type this. It's a warm day, but my office is on the shady side of the house, and typing doesn't exactly get your blood stirring. The heat generated by authorship is all in your head. It doesn't do much for your torso.

Don't look to fiberpile for wind protection, because you'll be disappointed. That same permeability to the wind, though, gives the material its tremendous comfort range. And it's easy to put on a shell garment to keep the wind from roaring through the pile to your hide. There's no doubt that pile works marvelously well over a broad range of conditions and is remarkably versatile. So is its slicker-looking cousin, bunting. I can certainly commend pile to your attention for just about any backcountry pursuit. The price is surely right. Just remember that pile is a part of a system of insulation, and proceed accordingly.

I haven't mentioned vests as insulated outerwear, which they certainly are. And they're certainly deservedly popular, be they down or synthetic. Some even have the virtue of reversibility, so you can comply with the Blaze Orange requirements for hunting gear that most states impose with one side, and have another side for wearing to the grocery store. I like vests. They provide just that extra touch of warmth you may need on a cool day. They're versatile, too. Cover that vest with a PTFE shell parka, and you've added a lot of warmth to your torso, where it's needed—with little weight, no possibility of heavy sweating under your arms, and considerable freedom of movement.

Vests work best if they're reasonably snug, to keep air from circulating too much. After all, ventilation isn't much of a problem in a sleeveless garment. Also, the vest should be long enough to cover your kidneys and the small of your back. I'm partial to a fairly high collar that I can turn up (or that stands up normally) to keep my long neck cozy. Other than that, evaluate a vest just like you'd evaluate a jacket. Remember that the vests with a very light nylon shell, either in ripstop or taffeta, will stuff down much smaller if you plan to carry one in a pack for that little extra touch of warmth needed in the outback.

I'm not going to say any more about raingear here, and I'll hold off on mittens and hats for now, and pick them up later. They deserve more than just a paragraph in a general chat about clothing. But I can't resist mentioning that awareness of what's happening with your body, and proper management of your heat production, will do more to keep you warm, dry and comfortable than any amount of sophisticated clothing. Remember Charley and Ed? Sure, some of their clothing was primitive and they didn't show much foresight in what they brought as back-up gear. Yet with any common sense at all, the worst they would have been was mildly uncomfortable. But even mildly uncomfortable is uncomfortable enough to blow that one good shot you get each season. So listen and learn. An ounce of smarts is worth a pound of gear — but the combination of the knowledge and the gear pretty much insures that you'll be ready and alert when you have to be.

Chapter 6
Sleeping Warm and Dry

Some people who spend a lot of time in the outdoors have never slept out a single night. Others sleep out only if they have to, to be near hunting and fishing hotspots. Others, like me, simply like to mess around in the woods and on rivers a lot, and spend a lot of time in a sleeping bag.

So you had your fill of that in the Army, or in the Scouts. Or the time you and your buddy walked back into some high country trout ponds and it rained for one day and dipped down below freeezing the next. None of you are ever going to do it again, if you live to be a thousand.

Well, you have my sympathy. You'll miss a lot. Just wandering around out there gives you a feeling for terrain and habitat that can serve you extremely well in hunting season. A quiet canoe trip can tell you a lot about a river, even if you didn't even bother to bring a rod. By the time you've put a canoe through fifteen or twenty splashy, cobbled rapids, you'll have a pretty fair idea of where the deep water lies that holds fish, and where it doesn't. You don't have to sleep cold, or be uncomfortable, to do it. Sure, tents and sleeping bags aren't being given away by your outfitter, but they're not that expensive in terms of the number of nights of use you'll get out of them. They also will extend your time afield.

Up outside North Hudson, in the heart of the Adirondacks, there's a small river that runs back into a ridge and valley system. The fishing's not bad where it's accessible, but a five-mile walk puts you in some excellent native brook trout water. You can bet your last #16 Quill Gordon that you won't find too many people in there fishing. Unfortunately, five miles in means five miles out, too. Even if you're a strong walker, that's four hours because the terrain isn't exactly paved. Not tough, but not a stroll in the park. Yet that little river is easy to fish if you take a pleasant stroll in on a Saturday morning, fishing your way up, make camp in the early afternoon, snooze, fish the evening, fish again the next morning, walk out, fishing as you go, snooze again for an hour, catch the evening hatch down by the road where the river gets big, and go home. Neat. Fun. Easy.

Fifteen pounds of gear is about all you'd need. If you're going with a friend, all you'll need more than what you're carrying is another sleeping bag, another foam pad, a couple more meals, and an additional coffee cup and bowl.

The key to this sort of mini-expedition to the hot spots is the sleeping bag and pad system you choose and how you use it. It's even more important than the tent. A good tent is a joy. It's dry, free from bugs, light, stable even in a wind, and easy to pitch. But you can get by with an eight by ten foot plastic tarp, if that's what you can afford. The bugs will love you for it, but once you're in that sleeping bag, with a headnet to keep the little bastards out of your nose, ears and mouth, you'll be comfortable enough. It's not the Conrad Hilton, nor some ancient fly fisherman's inn on a British chalk stream, but it'll do if your sleeping bag and pad keep you warm, dry and cozy, and you don't pitch your shelter in the middle of a natural bathtub.

Let's start with some hard data. The Army tells us that an inch of insulation will buy a sleeping person 40° of protection. In other words, that inch of insulation protects your 98.6° F minus 40° F, or 58.6° F. Two inches of insulation buys you another 40° — or warmth to 18.6° F.

I don't presume to argue with the Army. They have, after all, a pretty imposing bank of data from which to operate. But I do suspect that there's a substantial difference in comfort between what I call warm enough to be comfortable and what they call warm enough to be an effective combat infantryman. So let's arbitrarily say that one inch of insulation will buy you 27° of protection. Now, that two inches of insulation on top of you only buys you warmth to 44.6° F. Hmmm. Not quite enough for a fall hunt in the Rockies. Not nearly enough for a winter deer hunt. Barely enough for fishing in the Northeast in July, if the weather turns nippy. Try another inch, though, and you're down to 17.6° F. Okay. This means you'll be on the warm side for summer use, but you'll be just fine in all but the severest weather. There are ways to grab a few more degrees of protection that can make that sleeping bag good to well below zero.

When you look for a bag, though, don't look for one with three inches of thickness, or "loft", as the trade would have it. Look for a six-inch thick bag, because the industry tends to measure the overall thickness rather than the thickness of one side of a sleeping bag. There are a few exceptions. Some models may, for example, be four inches thick on one side and two on the other, so you can flip them over for warm nights or cold nights. The idea behind this is simple: you'll be sleeping on an insulated pad of some sort to keep you warm from the bottom, and the insulation of the bag that's under you will compress to a negligible thickness. It's what's on top that counts, to paraphrase an old ad jingle.

That's an oversimplification, but a useful one on which to base the selection of a sleeping bag. What you're really buying is a sleeping system, though. That system includes bag, foam pad, and shelter, be that shelter a tent, a bivouac sack into which you slide the sleeping bag, or a plain old tarp. It may even include a vapor barrier liner for the bag. But it still begins with the bag — and with a real-world appraisal of what you'll be doing with the bag.

What do I mean by a real-world appraisal? Simple. Figure out what you'll realistically be doing, and buy a bag that works for those conditions. Sure, you may go deer hunting for a week at a pop, but you stay in a hunting camp with some friends. Now, if it's like the hunting camps I'm accustomed to, a sleeping bag is rather more than a luxury. It's a downright necessity, if you'll pardon the pun. However, even if it's below zero outside, chances are that it won't be much below freezing inside, even if you forgot to get up at three o'clock and feed the oil barrel stove. So, you don't have to drop a lot of money on a sub-zero bag for deer hunting.

In fact, if most of us were really honest with ourselves, and separated out our dreams from what will really happen, we wouldn't buy a winter bag on the off-chance that someday, somehow, we were going into the Canadian barrenlands hunting polar bear. We'd buy what we needed to do the job at hand, and save our pennies so that someday we could take that once-in-a-lifetime trip. Then get that winter bag. Believe me, I'm not a lover of the Spartan approach. I work too damn hard for my bucks to want to throw them away, but I also work to buy the leisure time I crave. I'll keep that old car running long past its designed life span to have the cash available to take advantage of the opportunity to go fly fishing for bonefish in the Keys.

You won't have that cash available if you overbuy, or if you buy junk that has to be replaced or upgraded regularly. So let's start with a sleeping bag that works and doesn't cost an arm and a leg. The place to start is at your friendly local backpacking shop. This figures. True, it may not be run by Good-ol'-Johnny-who-cuts-you-a-deal-on-guns. Very likely, it's run by somebody who doesn't care a damn about the traditional field sports. But you can bet it's run by somebody who knows a great deal about backcountry camping gear, and who cares that you get the right gear for the job. These folks aren't usually into the deal-cutting side of the trade. The quality gear they buy doesn't give them the margin to cut deals. If you're a real scumbag you can take up their time and pick their brains for information, and try to cut a deal elsewhere that'll save you ten bucks. I've had it happen to me when I was an outfitter. That's not the way to work. These folks are pros who deal with a seemingly endless variety of gear and have selected the best they can find at several price points. It's worth the few bucks more you may—note that *may*—have to pay for their advice. As a regular customer of theirs, you can be assured that if they manage to get a really good deal from a supplier, you'll be the first to know. As specialists they'll stand behind what you buy. They need your good will and your repeat business.

End of sermon. On to sleeping bags.

It's a temptation to tell you to start with a down bag, but if I can't resist that temptation, you should unless you plan to do a lot of walking with a pack, toting that bag up hill and across valley and through swamp. In terms of warmth per unit weight, and in terms of compressibility, nothing comes close to a good down bag. Yes, it will lose insulation value if it gets damp, and it's worse than useless if it gets wet, for you'll never be able to dry it in the field. It's fearfully expensive, but there's still nothing like if if you do a lot of traveling on foot or in a canoe.

The synthetic bags aren't all that bad, though. Some are terrible, in all honesty, but the quality makers of backpacking bags are very reliable producers of gear that's worth the money. They have to be. You don't go out and buy a new sleeping bag every six months. When you make that purchase, you think about it and you look around. This means that the manufacturer had better be on his toes, and turn out gear that represents very good value for the money.

Expect quality. Also expect to pay for it, as you would for any other long-term investment. But first, learn to recognize quality when you see it.

Begin with a sleeping bag that's in the appropriate warmth category, slip off your shoes, and try it on. Try on several while you're at it. If you're not accustomed to sleeping bags, the more efficient mummy shapes may feel a bit confining at first. You'll soon get comfortable in them. A hint here to keep in mind is that you turn over with the bag, not inside the bag — as you would with a big, square-cut sleeper.

How do you know if the bag fits? Comfort is subjective. What feels good to you may not to me. However, you should be able to draw the hood up to its snuggest, and still have room at the bottom of the bag for your feet. You don't want to have your feet pressing against the foot of the bag, since you'll compress some of the insulation. Your feet will get cold. Up at the other end, you should have enough room in the hood and across the chest and shoulders that you're not compressing the insulation, too. Room enough. But not too much room. If the bag fits like an aircraft hangar, you'll have to warm all that moving air while you sleep—and some of that air will find its way out of the bag. With even the most elaborate of sleeping bags, it's inevitable that you'll lose some heat. Being in an overly large bag merely accelerates that loss.

I'm not going to subject you to the debate between chopped staple insulation (*Hollofil II* and *Quallofil*) and continuous filament insulation (*PolarGuard*). With all due respect to the makers of the fibers, and to the equipment builders, I'm not sure that the differences matter that much in terms of keeping you warm. The differences certainly pale into insignificance next to the differences in sleeping bag construction and design. For the record, though, *PolarGuard,* because it is provided in a continuous batt, is easier to keep in place with minimal stitching than its rivals. In theory, at least, there should be fewer cold spots with *PolarGuard.* The chopped staples need a little more care in sewing, to keep them where they'll do the most good. On the other hand, the chopped staple has a nicer feel and drape that the continuous filament, and the newest DuPont fiber, *Quallofil,* is marvelously compressible as well. In fact, *Quallofil* is potentially air-transportable, which means that it can be handled, and blown into tubes, just like down. This opens up all sorts of interesting possibilities for future development of very light-weight, efficient synthetic bags. As of right now, though, the manufacturers using it are treating it as a lighter *Hollofill II.* Rumors abound.

There are valid problems with a chopped staple as opposed to a continuous filament. Chopped staple migrates almost as easily as down; so it needs to be confined to relatively small tubes. This is okay, although it does tend to inhibit the loft of the material a bit. However, unlike down, chopped staple tends to clump and it's difficult to get the stuff dispersed back into place again. I haven't had this happen to any of my chopped staple gear, but maybe that's because I don't wash it as frequently as some folks do — certainly not as frequently as the standard wash resistance tests that most manufacturers conduct.

Continuous filament fiberfill, on the other hand, while a bit heavier per unit thickness, and a bit less compressible, tends to hold its form well, and lends itself to somewhat simpler construction. You pays your money and takes your choice.

Some things shouldn't be left to choice. The bag should fit, as we talked about earlier. There should be a generously wide draft tube behind the zipper, to keep the chilly winds out. At the foot of the zipper, check carefully to see that there are no openings through which heat can escape. This sounds like a silly injunction, but if you look at a lot of sleeping bags, you'll find many that have what could only be called stupidly designed draft tubes at the foot of the zipper.

If you want the bag to have a broad temperature range through which it's comfortable, make sure that the bag you buy has a so-called "double bug" zipper that can be opened from the foot on up on a warm night. Conversely, make sure that there's a *Velcro* tab at the head of the zipper to keep it from sliding open as you toss and turn on a cold night. Also check out the hood closure and shoulder closure drawcords. Some of them are so cunningly placed that you can't avoid chewing on them in your sleep.

Some frills are useful. Several manufacturers have draft collars in their bags to retain every last vestige of heat on a cold night. Some offer bags that can be augmented with a zip-on top layer of insulation, thus converting a 20° F bag to a 5° F bag for a reasonable price. Some others offer complete sleeping bag systems, consisting of an inner bag and an outer bag, which, when put together, add up to a deep winter bag. The commonest way to set up such a system is to build it around a basic three-season mummy bag that's warm, say, to about 20° F, and offer a larger, modified mummy bag that's warm to about 40° —45° F to put around it. This is a neat setup. Use the big, roomy outer bag for warm nights in the summer, and have the three-season bag for the chilly nights. Then, when the snow blows, put 'em both together. You have an arctic sleeper at about the all-up price of the arctic bag, but with a lot more flexibility. It's a little more cumbersome to pack, because you have to contend with more zippers and more fabric, but you can't have everything.

Of course, this is the sort of system that you can put together over a few years, or you can build from what you already have. If you have a decent, fairly roomy summer-weight bag, you're halfway there. Just take it with you to your outfitter's, and find a warmer bag that fits inside it.

While we've talked about some general principles for bag selection, we haven't really gotten down to the nitty and the gritty. You'll find, in your search for a bag, that seemingly similar bags differ in price by up to 35%. That's a lot of money!

What explains such a dramatic difference in cost? A lot of things. Let's assume, to simplify things a bit, that the bags are both the same thickness. Chances are that the cheaper bag is a bit snugger in certain places. This means that the manufacturer didn't have to use quite as much material. If you can live with the snugness, fine.

But that's just nickel and dime stuff. Material costs are far less important than labor costs, although the cheap bag maker takes every edge he can get. The inner and outer shells of the bag probably look just like The High Priced Spread. They're nylon taffeta, with a nominal weight of 2.2 ounces per square yard. But if you look at the fabric under a magnifying glass, or more specifically, that wondrous little learning tool called a thread counter, you'll find out that what looks alike isn't always alike. Hmmm. There seems to be fewer threads per inch in the cheap bag's fabric. Hmmm. A whole lot fewer. How about that!

Now this doesn't mean that the low-priced bag will immediately fall apart. It does mean that it won't take the beating over the long haul. That beating includes your washing machine.

How about the zippers? Well, the expensive bag has a double-bug separating YKK zipper. Fine. Nothing better. You can ventilate the bag from the foot on a hot night, and you can zip it to another bag of similar manufacture and have a backcountry nuptial couch. Okay! The cheap bag has a single-bug YKK of a slightly smaller size. A good zipper, to be sure, but it lacks the flexibility of the other zipper, and the strength.

How about the draft tube, that stuffed sausage behind the zipper that keeps the chilly air out and the warm air in? Hmmm. The cheap bag has one, but it's about the diameter of a healthy North American Brown water snake, and it doesn't go all the way to the foot of the bag. In fact, it ends right where the zipper ends, and there's a little opening below it. The draft tube on the good bag is about the size of a healthy rock python, and it goes all the way to the end of the bag.

How about the foot of the bag? Well, the cheap bag has a simple foot. It's well-enough designed, but if you put your size 12's against it, you push straight through to the outer layer of fabric. That's going to be nippy. On the other hand, the better bag has a complex foot, made up of a lot of little pieces, and you can push on them from now until hell freezes over without reaching that outer layer of fabric. Result? Warm feet.

In fact, the difference between a good draft tube and a well-cut foot versus a mediocre draft tube and a simple foot can account for

The Anatomy of a Sleeping Bag

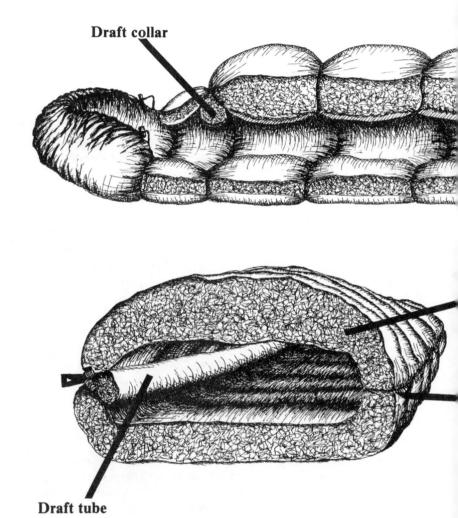

Draft collar

Draft tube

I-beam baffles

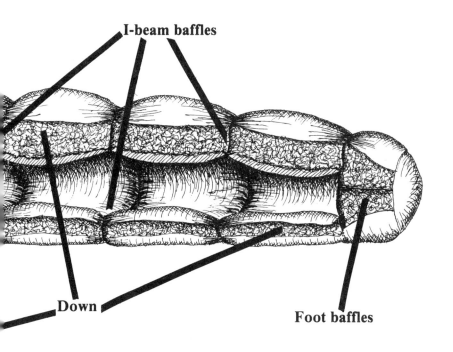

Down

Foot baffles

Cross block baffle

over forty bucks at retail all by themselves. The difference in warmth when you're working near the extreme range of the bag is significant.

If you turn the bag inside-out, you'll find that the low-priced bag has rough, unfinished seams, or bound seams at best. The good bag usually has taped seams, or very meticulously done bound seams. The difference is comfort and longevity.

If you keep looking, you'll find other differences. There usually aren't as many stitches per inch in a low-priced bag as in a quality bag. The stitchlines may be sloppy and crooked as well. This doesn't mean that the bargain bag builder hires incompetents, but it means that he's not as rigorous with inspection procedures.

Other niceties separate the real product from the imitation. Points of unusual stress and tension are reinforced in a good bag. Just like the quality parka has little bar tacks at the edges of the pockets to keep them from ripping loose, so the quality sleeping bag will have bar tacking where it counts, and an extra line of stitching at critical places like zippers.

The difference at any one point is generally insignificant, but the sum total of minor differences becomes a major difference in product usability and durability. And appearance, too. Appearance is window dressing, you say. But at its best, it isn't. Quality gear somehow looks like quality gear, even if it's notably free from bells and whistles and foxtails. But then again, the best fishing gear in the world is typically the simplest in appearance and the most unadorned. There aren't any jumping trout on a Hardy fly reel. The name is more than enough.

In a sense, the name is more than enough on most sleeping bags, too. The mainstream builders of gear for the backpacking trade are remarkably dependable in terms of quality and good value for the dollar. Not every bag they build is a super-fancy high-end sack, either. They're more than aware of a need for solidly made, well-designed middle priced equipment. And the magic name is still on it. These builders don't hide their midrange gear under a different label. You'll find the same quality and the same generous cut. What you won't find is the array of little extras that run the manufacturing time (and the cost) up.

Oddly enough, the synthetic bags seem to be more generously endowed with little goodies today than the down bags. It may simply be that the down bag is perceived as so expensive that to add to the cost by adding extras would result in a dramatic loss of market. Actually the down bag stands in just about the same price relationship to the synthetic bag that it did years ago when high-grade well-designed synthetic fill bags became established in the market.

I said that I wasn't going to talk much about down bags at the beginning of this chapter, because I felt that down bags were something in the way of an extravagance for people who didn't really need a maximum weight to warmth ratio. But over the years, I've found that once people are convinced through their own experience that they can be comfortable in the backcountry, they start hiking and paddling and even snowshoeing and cross-country skiing just for the sake of the activities themselves. You'll know when you're hooked. I realized it when I found myself wandering through the hills behind the house in the fall without my 16 double under one arm. No, I didn't quit bird hunting. But I didn't need the gun as a visible excuse for being out there. As it went, I think I learned more about partridge when I wasn't hunting them than when I was!

When you get to that point, you'll start thinking about a down bag. Yeah, I can give you four hundred cogent reasons why neither you nor I really need one, and why that small weight saving and size saving in your pack that a down bag gives you isn't that all-fired important. But there are things that numbers capture poorly, if at all. A great canoe, a fine fly rod, a well-balanced shotgun—the essence is rather more than the sum of their specifications. Somehow, down just plain feels right. It forms around you and fills up the cold little spaces, and it moves out of the way when you want it to move. It *fits*, in short. Sure, it loses efficiency when it's damp, and it's useless when wet. But you can combat dampness, and you're not supposed to tip your canoe over in the first place. It never hurts us to live with a material that has a few built-in liabilities. It may teach us something.

I was taught bait casting by an old man who used a free-spool reel without a level-wind mechanism and without the slightest hint of an anti-backlash device. It took me a long time to learn, but I think I was a better bait caster because of it. And I look on my free-spool reel, which has a level-winder, and feel somehow soft and housebound. The old habits die hard. Level-winder or no, I still palm the reel on a retrieve and run the line through the thumb and forefinger of my left hand. It doesn't feel right any other way.

A down bag is much the same. You learn the little rituals for keeping it absolutely dry. In time, the rituals take on a meaning of their own, and provide a tangible link with your past. We need these links. We glory in them. Is there any good reason for the ritual cleaning of a shotgun after a fall afternoon bird hunt? Not really, in these days of smokeless powders, non-corrosive primers, and tenacious lubricants. Except it's what you do after a hunt. You sit around the kitchen table, drink coffee, talk, and clean your shotgun. Later that night you touch up the waterproofing on your boots.

In the same way, you lovingly spread out your down bag in the morning sun to dry it while you drink your coffee. You get up once to turn it, settle down, have another cup of coffee, think about breakfast, and watch the country awaken. When you pack up to go, you make sure that the bag is well tucked into its stuff sack, and stowed neatly in your pack. By then it's time for one last cup of coffee, perhaps a pipeful of tobacco, and some quiet contemplation on a job well done, a debt paid.

But it still helps to have a good down bag to begin with. The usage criteria are the same, of course: temperature range and fit. Evaluation criteria are a bit more complex in some ways because you have no way of knowing the quality of down used in the bag. You do have to place a bit of faith in the manufacturer's reputation. Again, down is a luxury item. The general quality level is high among the better-known makers. As you might expect, there are some small shops in the trade that offer bags so well designed and so well made that it seems almost sinful to sleep in them.

Let's begin with the obvious—the fabric shell of the down bag. Down is funny stuff. It's a collection of tiny pods, "plumules" in the trade, that look like nothing so much as fuzzy parachutes. Mixed in with these are some small feathers, the size and quantity of which is one of the determiners of the grade of down. High-quality fill has fewer, smaller feathers. No down is completely free of them, and there are some sleeping bag builders who feel that this is all to the good. That small quantity of tiny feathers will act as little paddles and keep the down from clumping. Whether this is simply making a virtue of an inevitability or not, I frankly don't know. However, there are a lot of little, shifty things running around inside a down bag. They all want to get out. This means that the fabric used to cover a down bag must be very tightly woven; otherwise these little buggers will leak out through the weave of the fabric. It's easy to spot a down bag made with a loose weave. It looks like it's growing a crop of tiny gray seedlings. In even the best bags, you may find an occasional feather poking through, but you shouldn't find something that looks like a lawn of fungus in dire need of mowing.

Conversely, the fabric shouldn't be so tightly woven as to effectively shut off the transmission of moisture-laden warm air to the outside. In other words, the bag has to breathe. Yet if it breathes too much, it'll leak down plumules.

Most down bags are covered with very light fabric, ranging from

1.9 and 2.2 ounces per yard all the way down to around one ounce per yard. In other words, down bags aren't meant to be used as wrestling mats. Neither are good synthetic bags, for that matter, although the synthetics are usually covered with a 2.2 ounce fabric, because the slight additional weight of the fabric will have little or no effect on the loft of the material. On the other hand, too heavy a shell fabric can inhibit the loft of down. And it adds to the weight of the bag. How much? Not a lot. A few ounces in weight and a few cubic inches in compressibility; that's all. But when you're toting it, a few ounces and a few cubic inches saved here and there makes a few pounds very quickly. And down bags are made for people who'll be toting their gear.

If fabric is one of the differences that's readily apparent in the construction of a down bag, the next obvious difference is that down needs to be restrained in relatively small pockets if the insulation blanket over you is to be uniformly maintained. In a jacket, it's acceptable to stitch through the fabric and make little tubes for the down. Sure, there's some heat loss at the stitchlines, but in severe conditions, you can overcome a lot of that loss by wearing a shell garment. And you're generally moving when you're wearing a parka. Your heat production is high. When you're sleeping, though, your heat production is low. You can't afford to lose heat, however small the amount may be. Synthetic bags may be sewn through, but there's a thickness of insulation between the stitchlines. I'ts common practice to interlayer a free-floating insulation batt between the stitched layers on the inside and outside of the top of the bag. This eliminates cold spots fairly well. You don't have that option with down, unless you're building a superlight sewn-through bag that will be used by itself only in warm weather, and used in cold weather as an inner bag in a two bag sleeping system.

The commonest way for the down bag designer to eliminate cold spots and insure uniform insulation thickness is to design a bag with slanted rectangular tubes to contain the down in the body area. This construction is called *slant box* or *offset box* construction. A somewhat simpler structure, but with the seams aligned top and bottom, is called a *box* or an *I-beam*. Rabid backpackers have been known to engage in physical violence over the differences. In theory, the slant box offers better control of the down, because the down in one tube tends to both restrain and support the down in the adjacent tubes. I suspect that the theory is correct. As to how much difference it makes, I don't know. There are other variables that impinge: the amount and the quality of the down fill, the baffle material that runs from the top shell to the bottom shell and provides the "sidewalls" for the compartments, the width of the tubes, and the cut of the bag itself.

The amount and the quality of the down fill makes an enormous difference, of course. Well-filled down compartments don't permit as much down migration, and high-quality down simply fills the compartment better with less material. This should be obvious.

The baffle material is less obvious. A slippery nylon marquisette netting may discourage the down plumules from sticking to it, while a soft, stretchy circular knit material conforms better to the shape of the bag when it's in use and tends to keep the plumules snuggled up against it, insuring a more even distribution.

Tube width, which you can check easily since it's the distance between stitchlines, is critical. In general, the narrower the tubes, the easier it is to control the down. Six inch tubes are fine; four inch tubes are unusual, and even better; eight-inchers will work if the fill is good, and the maker didn't skimp on the quantity. Anything much more than that is unacceptable.

Tube width is one place where the good and the mediocre are obviously at variance. For example, a bag that's 72 inches long to the foot section would contain twenty baffles (ten on top, ten on the bottom) if it has six-inch tubes. That same bag with nine-inch tubes would only contain twelve baffles. That's sixteen fewer stitchlines that have to be sewn, and eight fewer pieces of material that have to be cut. Take it further. If the six-inch tube bag has slant wall tubes, and the nominal thickness of the bag is eight inches overall (four inches per "side"), each baffle has to be at least six inches deep plus seam allowance. If the cheaper bag has the same thickness, but is cut as an I-beam rather than a slant wall, the baffles only have to be four inches deep, plus seam allowance. The maker of the better bag, therefore, will use nearly three times the amount of baffle material in his bag. In the body alone! This doesn't begin to take into account that the better bags usually have elaborate hoods and foot sections that are a cutting room foreman's nightmare and a machine operator's horror movie. Little subtleties like this result in a huge price differential.

The cut of the bag itself is another one of those lovely theoretical tempests in a teacup. Down is compressible. This is both its glory and its bane. Stick a knee up against a sleeping bag, and that knee can displace down, leaving that knee insulated from the chills of winter by two layers of 1.5 ounce per yard ripstop nylon and twelve hardnosed down pods that wouldn't be displaced. To get around this, most sophisticated sleeping bags are cut in such a way that all the pushing in the world will still keep that knee insulated. It's called *differential cut,* which simply means that the outer shell of the sleeping bag is significantly wider than the inner shell to make insulation displacement difficult. As long as you're in the bag, there is no way that you can push the inner shell up to the outer. The bag maker consequently has to cut two different patterns, which takes more time, and which may leave some scrap of a size he can't use for stuff bags and such. It costs more to make a differentially cut bag . And if it costs more, you'll pay more.

The same holds true for hoods and foot sections. The better the insulation layer is maintained, and the more real (as opposed to theoretical) room you have, the more costly the bag will be. Years ago one manufacturer told me that eliminating that nagging little opening at the foot of the zipper, and backing it with a draft tube in a workmanlike manner, cost him five bucks. That was nine years ago. Right now, the cost would be closer to fifteen bucks. You can double that by the time it gets to you, because both the manufacturer and the retailer have to make a living.

But that's not all. Typically, a sleeping bag is made in two halves and joined at the side, although some bags use a one-piece outer shell (top and bottom) and stitch into it. Where the pieces join at the sides is a problem. There isn't much room to sew in there, and you're working with miserable little pieces. There's a lot of cutting time and needle time involved. Some builders simply say, "To hell with it", and sew the halves together in what could best be called a fat sewn-through seam that leaks heat like a half-opened faucet leaks water. Other builders simply run the down tubes all around the bag—a common solution in a square-cut bag, or any bag in which the zipper runs clear around the bottom of the foot section so it can be opened as a quilt. This isn't bad, but that's still a lot of room for those slippery little down pods to roam in. While it's a lot better than the sewn-through side seam, it's not optimum.

The best bags use what's called a *cross block baffle,* a piece of baffle material that keeps the down in the half of the bag where it belongs and also maintains full tube thickness at the sides of the bag. It's sort of like having your cake and eating it too. Needless to add, this little bit of needlework witchery increases the manufacturing cost more than a little bit. It certainly increases the warmth of the bag by a fair chunk.

Other than the major design features, a down bag is still needlework, and a part of its value lies in the quality of the sewing. Is it clean, tidy and workmanlike? Are the seams taped? Are there loose ends of thread and tag ends of fabric sticking out, or is everything shipshape? Are there somewhere between ten and twelve stitches per inch, or are there great, huge six-stitch-per-inch seams that'll snag on everything? These things are simple to evaluate. In a sense it's no different than looking over a new shirt.

But the best sleeping bag in the world, laid out lovingly inside the best tent in the world, will still give you a cold night's sleep.

I remember a guy who came into my shop regularly, mostly browsing around. Pleasant guy. Did some backcountry fishing and a little bit of hunting, and seemed generally to know what he was talking about. He bought a sleeping bag from me, a big Gerry Himalayan, a model no longer made. It was a monster. I had a few in rental, and I found that I was too warm in the bag at -20° F — and I'm a cold sleeper.

Well, he came back after a warm fall weekend complaining bitterly about the bag. After I talked to him a bit, and got him calmed down, I found out that he'd gone to bed exhausted, wearing his sweat-soaked clothing, and although he was too tired to eat, he managed to knock down about five fingers of sour mash. He simply threw his bag on the ground, on top of a small tarp, and went to sleep.

There, in one short paragraph, is how not to keep warm in the outdoors. His sweaty clothes fairly sucked heat out of him, and got the sleeping bag wet to boot, which helped the heat loss along. He wasn't producing much heat, because he was chilled and tired, and badly in need of food. He was probably dehydrated, and helped that along by knocking down some booze. Of course, the booze dilated his blood vessels, which increased his heat loss, and it triggered a dump of glycogens from his liver which were probably his last easily-accessible supplies of energy. To compound that, he slept on the ground with no insulation under him except a thin nylon tarp and some squashed down pods. He was a big man, but in a contest between a 220 pounder at 98.6° F and many tons of world at rather less, you know who's going to lose the heat loss war. It could have been worse. But mercifully, it didn't rain.

Body management plays a part in keeping warm. If you remember those rules laid down years ago by Velocio, the French writer on bicycling, they all deal, in one way or another, with body management. In more straightforward terms, you'll sleep cold if you go to bed hungry, and you'll sleep even colder if you go to bed thirsty. Dehydration can be a discomfort in summer. In blazing hot weather, it can be fatal, as it can be in winter. Tank up. Sure, this may mean an unscheduled trip to the nearest bush at two in the morning, but that's a small price to pay for comfort. Beside, you can shoo away the raccoons while you're out.

In cold weather a couple of cups of sweetened tea go down well before bedtime. I've even taken a candy bar or some such munchie into the tent in winter and washed it down with water after my inevitable early morning constitutional.

I'm about the last person on earth who'll go on a tirade about booze. I don't think it has any place around firearms, and I still like the old idea I grew up with: you unlock the liquor cabinet only after you've locked the gun case. But after a day in the outback, what some of my Southern friends would call a "shooter" of Scotch mixed with a touch of branch water doesn't go down badly at all. If you're warm and cozy to begin with, that is. If you're chilled to the bone, eat and drink, but keep the drinking to water, tea, coffee or cocoa, please. Booze does you no good then, and may make you only colder. You'll notice that all these old boys who talk about "warming up" with three fingers of Three Feathers do it when they're back home, sitting in front of a warm stove. They're not doing it at streamside when they're shivering.

You can still be the model of cold water propriety, eat well, change into dry clothes, and all those other good things, and still freeze your butt off. All you have to do is sleep on the ground. Again, there's no way you can win the heat loss war with Mother Earth.

Any insulation that's compressible enough to be packed easily, even in the back of a four-wheeler, is compressible enough to lose most, if not all, of its insulation ability when its compressed by the weight of a sleeping body. You need supplemental insulation under you, for both warmth and comfort. And you can get this in several ways.

The old standby is the air mattress. It's comfortable, but because the air inside it actually circulates, and transfers heat away from your body, it's not the warmest of options. And it's a good bit less than useless when it gets punctured in the middle of the night. Granted, the contemporary air mattress is pretty tough and reliable, but there's still the problem of warmth. If all your camping will be in the summer, there's no problem, but if you plan to do any late fall or winter camping, I'd consider something warmer.

The warmer option is a foam pad. These come in three basic types. Commonest is the open-cell foam pad, covered with water-proof nylon on the bottom to keep it dry, and covered with a polyester/cotton on the top to keep you from slipping around on it as you sleep. They're comfortable, quite warm, and a bit bulky, especially in the full-length versions.

An alternative, and the commonly-used pad of the winter camper, is a somewhat thinner pad of closed-cell foam. The closed-cell foam pad is less comfortable, being both thinner and far less compressible, but its insulation value is very high.

The luxury alternative is an open-cell foam pad with a completely waterproof cover and an air valve that's marketed under the name of *Therm-A-Rest*. It's warm (because the foam restrains the circulation of air) comfortable, packs into a small bundle for easy transport, and it's fiercely expensive. I think I'd go camping without mine if the choice was to go without or to stay home, but I'd bitch and fuss all the time. Addictive!

As I grow older, grayer, and spindlier in the shanks, I like the creature comfort provided by a full-length sleeping pad. However, I've slept many nights on the short "backpacking length" pads, which usually run about 42 inches long. Just slide a pack or your raingear under your feet, and you're cozy in most weather, and you'll be carrying a lighter, tidier, less expensive pad.

A few more pointers before we move on. All the books say to sleep naked in your sleeping bag. This is fine if you like it. If you don't, wear something. You won't be breaking the Law of the Backcountry if you do.

Consider also that clothing can greatly extend the range of your bag. Dry socks, dry long johns, and a wool cap can turn a 15° F bag into a zero bag. And if you toss your insulated parka over the bag (not under; over), you can add even more warmth.

There are other ways to extend the range of your bag. An obvious one is the use of a vapor barrier liner. The VBL can offer a dramatic improvement in bag performance by simply cutting down on the moisture you pump into your insulation when you sleep. Add to this an overshell of a coated nylon or PTFE (*Gore-Tex* or *Klimate*), and you have a bag that's essentially sealed against moisture from within and without that's well protected against wind loss as well. With this setup, sleeping under a tarp is comfortable — even in inclement weather.

Chapter 7

Tents

Staying warm and dry isn't much of a problem if you vacation in a cottage and never go outside when it's raining. But if you want to go into the backcountry for whatever reason for an extended period of time, keeping warm and dry poses more of a problem. It necessitates carrying some sort of shelter with you.

Back in the old days when the Faithful Guide carried the tent and whipped out his axe to erect a leanto on the spot for cooking and dining and casual conversation, life was a bit easier for all backwoods roamers. Today, unless you're a powerhouse writer who has his way paid by some million copy a month magazine, or you happen to own said magazine, you'll be doing what I do. You carry a tent with you. It had better be big enough for comfort, but it had better be light, too, unless you're a middle linebacker. Even if you're the strongest guy on the block, you're not out there for the exercise.

Take heart. There are many tents that are both roomy and light. And they do an admirable job of turning rain aside. Some of them are particularly well suited for winter as well. Yep, you can camp in the snow. You can even be comfortable in the snow. If you don't believe it, I invite you to make me a rich writer and get a copy of my *Movin' On: Equipment and Technique for Winter Hikers*. It's also published by the folks at Stone Wall Press.

Assuming you want to be truly dry and comfortable, let's eliminate a few shelters right off the bat. Tarps are fine if you're a masochist, but not if you want to be comfortable. They'll turn a rain, and I'm certain that somewhere some topological wizard has figured out a way to arrange one so it will turn wind-driven rain, but I'm not that guy. I've used tarps a lot. If you arrange one like a leanto, it's passable except in bug season. But not when the rain comes howling in — driven by a twenty mile per hour wind! No way!

Forget tarps. Forget also canvas wall tents and big canvas house tents. If you can carry one in with your four-wheeler and set it up as a base camp, I suppose it'd be fine. Until it rains for two days. Also forget any tent that requires a rat's nest of guy lines and nineteen stakes. I know that this category encompasses some fine tents, but let's keep your life simple.

Also, forget any tent that's made of a single layer of coated nylon. It'll leak unless you seal all the seams meticulously. Then it'll leak a little less. After you've resealed the seams, it won't leak until you sleep in it. At that point your breath will condense on the inside of the roof, and it'll leak from the inside in as opposed to from the outside in. This is small consolation.

What you'll be looking for is a double-walled tent that's mostly self-supporting without additional guy lines. A backpacking tent, in short. Now, this tent may look like the good old A-frame you used as a Scout, with the added fillip of a ridgepole that connects the front A-frame to the rear A-frame, or it could look like something out of *Star Wars.* Believe me, there are some dome tents on the market that are very handsome and very exotic. They look more like sculptures in fabric than tents. They're light, rigid in a wind, dry, roomy, and they're not cheap.

Why the double-wall tent? Easy. The double-wall tent (or the tent with a fly, if you prefer) is a structure with a waterproof floor, waterproof sidewalls up a foot or so, and a body that isn't waterproof. Over this is fitted a waterproof fly, at a sufficient distance above the permeable tent body to provide for a good flow of air. Moisture—that insensible perspiration that happens just because you're alive, and water vapor from your breath—passes through the permeable tent wall and condenses on the fly, from which it runs down harmlessly to the ground.

Mostly. In the real world out there, the proper combination of temperature and moisture could result in condensation forming on cheesecloth. I remember one night like that very vividly. We were camped on Rabbit Key in the Everglades, out in the Gulf, and it was warm. Of course it was also damp. I was using a tropical tent, a double-wall, ridgepoled A-frame with a mesh body rather than a ripstop nylon body. It was a gin-clear night, so I left the fly off to watch the stars. On a clear night, the Gulf Coast sky is unbelievably beautiful. What a fine way to drop off to sleep after a good day of paddling.

The next morning my bag was damp, and there was a gentle trickle of condensate running off the mesh body of the tent. The other folks on the trip, who left their tent flies in place, really got soaked. So, with the right combination of temperature and humidity, you still get some condensation, even in a tent that's mostly holes.

At present there is a vast and bewildering array of cheap tents on the market. Most of them look like they were subcontracted to the

Dome Tent

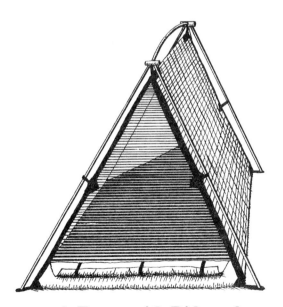

A-Frame with Ridgepole

chimps at the Bronx Zoo by a greedy contractor in Hong Kong who felt that the going labor rate there was far too high. The designs aren't always bad, because anybody can steal a design. But the fabric, the reinforcement, the zippers and the sewing are pure schlock.

The kind of junk is easy to pass by. What's more difficult to determine is why one tent sells for $140 and one that looks just like it sells for $120. It's obvious to everybody that if they were exactly the same, then somebody's pricing is way out of line. A closer look will tell you that they're not the same. Let's take two popular two-person tents of similar appearance and dimensions, separated in price by a few bucks, and see where the differences lie.

Tent A	Tent B
1. Straight cut roofline.	1. Contoured roofline. Uses more fabric but gives more headroom.
2. Composite door and screen. Screen in front of door.	2. Separate door and screen. Door in front of screen for better protection. More ventilation area.
3. Two full length floor seams.	3. One full-length floor seam.
4. One unbound mesh pocket.	4. Two bound mesh pockets.
5. 1.9 oz., 74 thread per inch fabric; may vary.	5. 1.9 oz., 98 threads per inch fabric, treated with ultraviolet inhibitor.
6. Poles: ½ inch O.D., 033 wall.	6. 5/8 inch O.D. poles, .035 wall.
7. 1/16 inch shock cord.	7. 3/8 inch shock cord.
8. Average 7-8 stitches per inch in seams.	8. Average 8-10 stitches per inch in seams.
9. Edge of fly turned and hemmed with a single needle stitch.	9. Edges of fly bound with nylon tape and double needle stitched.
10. Corner pullouts not reinforced; attached with a zigzag backstitch.	10. Corner pullouts reinforced with 8 oz. packcloth and bar tacked.
11. Tent corners reinforced with 1.9 oz. fabric.	11. Tent corners reinforced with 8 oz. packcloth.
12. Tent bag of 1.9 oz. nylon.	12. Tent bag of 8 oz. pack cloth.

The suggested retail of Tent A is within twenty dollars of Tent B. Tent A, however, is frequently discounted, and may be up to forty dollars cheaper. I'll leave it to you to determine what's the better long-term value. But I won't leave you without a little sermon. If you're going to use a tent once a year, Tent A is more than good enough. It's not Tent B, but it far surpasses the junk often found at "bargain" prices. And it manifestly does the job. It works well. It'll keep you warm and dry, given reasonable care. If you plan to use the tent more frequently, there's something to be said for the generally more robust construction of Tent B. The choice is yours.

In the long run, though, for me to tell you that there are construction differences between tents of different prices isn't telling you much that you don't know already. However, the differences pointed out above are those places where differences most often appear. Extra needlework takes time, and time is money. Reinforcement patches may come from the scrap bag, but they still have to be cut to the proper shape and sewn in place. A complex door arrangement that provides positive weather protection, complete ventilation and easy access requires more sewing and more zippers. Even relatively simple tent poles can vary widely in cost, because the sturdier poles simply take more material to make. At the high end, you'll find tents offered with optional pole sets — a sturdy, fairly heavy fiberglass pole set, and a lightweight superalloy set that may well cost you one hundred dollars more. The strengths are similar; the weights may vary as much as two pounds. You can live with two pounds for occasional use, but not when you're carrying the tent on a severe mountaineering trip.

If you're aware of the differences, and where they most often occur, it can simplify your tent buying a great deal. That way you're free to determine your own trade-offs of quality versus cost. But there's one area where you shouldn't make any trade-offs. That's comfort. No small, readily transportable tent is ever much more than an opulent doghouse. Don't look for the comforts of home. Look for the comforts you absolutely need.

A reasonable amount of room is one comfort. It may be to your advantage to go to a three-person tent instead of a two-person tent if you get easily upset by confined spaces. Space alone does not make a tent comfortable. It helps, but all the room in the world is poor recompense for a door that's tough to get in and out of, too little ventilation, a fly that fits poorly and flaps in the wind, and doors cunningly engineered to let snow and rain in whenever you go in. The only way to find out about a tent is to live in it for a weekend— preferably a weekend that has some rain. Some better shops actually have tents you can rent, which is a worthwhile investment. Many times, if you come back and buy a tent from these folks, they'll refund your rental, which is certainly a good deal. I never did that. I figured that you should have to pay for what you learn, and renting a tent that you're thinking of buying is a helluva learning experience. But then I never said that I didn't have some strange ideas.

Barring the opportunity to rent, the best you can do is spend time lolling around in the tent on the outfitter's floor. This is best done with your tentmate, or with the whole family if they are the traveling companions of your choice.

Again, don't expect a lot of room. Tents made for backpackers and other wild country rovers are made for sleeping, not partying. The typical pattern of camp life usually keeps you outdoors and active until you nod over your teacup in front of the campfire and crawl into the sack. Even if it's raining, there's still something to do and somewhere to go, and you have good raingear to help you do just that. However, if you're well over six feet tall and the tent is a scant six feet long, you'll have some problems. The time to find that out is in the shop, not in the backcountry.

Okay, so the tent isn't exactly an executive suite in size, but it's large enough for sleeping. Now, can one person get up and leave the tent without stomping on someone's face? Can you get out of the door easily from the inside? Can you open the tent and the fly if it's a dome with a fly that has to be opened in a pouring rain without having your own private swimming pool inside the tent by the time you get in? Are there cunning little crannies that will hold snow, like around doors and vents? Can you pitch the thing without an engineering degree? Can you pitch it by yourself if you have to? In a wind? In the rain?

Give some hard thought to where you'll be using the tent. A lot of my camping is on bare rock along lakes and rivers. Some of it is on sand. Some is on tent platforms in swamps. None of these places will hold a stake worth a damn. I'm almost locked into the type of tent that's largely, if not totally, self-supporting. I also find that this type of tent is just about optimum for winter use, as well. True, you'll never make a tent completely stable in high winds without some additional guying, but most of us don't camp in very exposed places that are frequently swept by high winds.

If a lot of your camping is in places where you can push in a skinny wire stake without much trouble, you may not need the self-supporting tent at all. You can save yourself some money, in that case. In general, the self-supporting tents and the nearly self-supporting ones require complex patterns and elaborate poles. They're heavier than the standard A-frame tent, and more costly. Of course they're also a bit roomier. However, money is money, and the difference in cost could well be enough for a first-rate fly rod.

Finally, do you like being in the tent? Does it feel pleasant, or is it a bit claustrophobic? Is the color cheerful or depressing? I know that this sounds dumb, but it's a very important part of tent selection. If you don't like the color, and find the tent depressing, it can be the greatest tent in the universe, but you won't use it much. You might never figure out why. Fast food restaurant people spent a lot of time and money and research figuring out what color combinations induce folks to eat quickly, make room for others, but hurry back in the future.

For the go-light enthusiast, or for the person who may frequently go alone into the outback, there's a whole new generation of what I suppose could be called mini-tents that accommodate one or two people, and that weigh under four pounds. Some of these tents are little more than bivouac sacks with a little bit of headroom. Others are quite roomy, at least in terms of length and width, if not height. However, the current design trend is toward providing enough headroom to permit a tall person to sit up, and even to kneel. At least you can get your pants on without doing the upper-berth shuffle, and find something in your jacket pocket.

These tents make it possible, by the way, to maintain what I like to think of as a "Getaway Pack". This is a fairly good-sized rucksack that you can hang in a closet, and keep your sleeping gear, shelter, raingear, minimal cooking gear, and a few freeze-dried meals in, and grab on a moment's notice for a quick overnight or weekend trip. My "Getaway Pack" is an old ski touring rucksack with the pockets tacked down along the sides only, so you can slide skis behind them. I can't think of a better pack for backcountry fishing trips than this one. It's not big enough to live comfortably out of for a week, but for a quick overnight all I have to do is slip a rod or two behind those ski pockets, toss some tackle in the header pouch of the pack (or simply take my fishing vest), and I'm ready to go whenever I hear there's some action on the river.

Chapter 8
Comfortable Feet

In all my years in the back country, I've hardly ever heard a word about tired backs, aching shoulders, sore legs and such. But I've heard enough complaining about sore feet to fill a very large book.

I suppose that's to be anticipated. Most of us don't walk nearly as much as we should. Every now and then, I even catch myself driving a mile to the post office to pick up a magazine on running. Ridiculous! Yet we all yield to the pressures of time and drive when we know we'd be more fit if we walked. Consequently, we're out of shape and overweight. We walk like we're overweight, too. You know, back in an S-curve, legs apart, heels hammering into the ground. When weekends come, we expect to heave our bulk out of the car seat, and march over a few hills to find a wild turkey. Our training all week for this has been walking to the kitchen to find the Wild Turkey.

This is a tough situation for your feet. A hard walk in rough terrain is tough enough without complicating it by being out of shape, but we manage. Choosing shoes that simply don't do the job also don't help. In many cases, we're wearing shoes that don't even fit!

Let's start off by taking a good, close look at feet. If you know how they work, you'll be better prepared to help them work more comfortably.

If a boot is ever going to fit you, it must fit at certain key points of your foot. The first ones are the first and the fifth metatarsal heads, the areas just behind the big toe and the little toe, just where they flex. This is the widest part of the foot. Next is the longitudinal arch, which begins just ahead of the weight-bearing part of the heel and extends forward to a line across the metatarsal heads.

Next are two bones that form the ankle, and finally, the heel. To further muddy up the issue, there are four different "arches" that must be fitted. There is an arch across the instep and one across the metatarsals. There's a longitudinal arch that follows the big toe side of the foot, and a smaller arch along the outside of the foot. In other words, you're dealing with a very fragile bone structure that's remarkably flexible. There isn't a straight line in it.

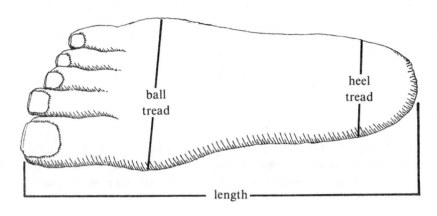

ball tread

heel tread

length

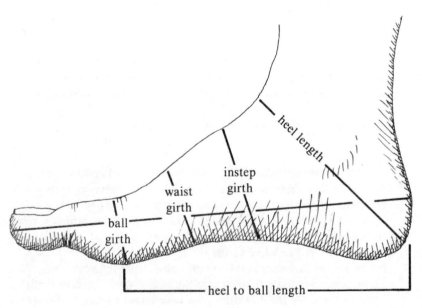

heel length

instep girth

waist girth

ball girth

heel to ball length

Fortunately, most human feet fall within fairly well-defined patterns in the critical areas, so it's possible to develop a foot form that will account for most variations. This foot form is called a "last". Its measurements are derived from a statistical survey of the critical dimensions of human feet.

It should be no surprise that the repository for such wisdom in America is the Army. After all, what group has had the occasion to fit more people with footgear? And if it wasn't fitted well, the blunder was probably that of the dude issuing the boots. The Army last, developed in the early years of the century by Dr. Munson, who was then Surgeon-General, has held up well as a foot form, subject to some modifications as we grew larger and longer-footed as a national group.

However ubiquitous the Munson last may be, you don't have to have a doctorate degree to know that boots from different makers fit differently. This is only in part a function of the last dimensions. Boots can alter in shape during finishing operations, and cheap leather changes dimension more than good leather. Further, each boot maker modifies a last a bit in accordance with what he sees to be his main market. Low-priced work boots are typically lasted on a wider heel than high-grade hunting boots, for example. It may be a simple accommodation to the quality of the leather, or it may be based on the assumption that most men who wear work boots are rather sturdier and broader of foot than men who buy very costly hunting boots. I don't know. But I've fitted a lot of boots in my day, and I've tried on a lot of boots — both for my own purchases and for my own information as an outfitter.

A lot of folks ask me, "What kind of boot should I buy?" All I can tell them is to buy a boot that fits them. When pressed for a brand name recommendation, I have to merely shrug and plead ignorance. I have to here, too. I'm not you. I'm probably built differently, I walk differently, my feet are not like yours — there are a myriad of reasons why I can't tell you what boot to buy. I can tell you whose boots I think are very well made. I can tell you whose boots are lasted in such a way that they're an easy fit in a shop for most people. But that's all I can tell you about the boots themselves. So—when your buddy tells you that you should buy a pair of so-and-so's because they really fit well, thank him for his advice, but take his recommendation with a grain of salt.

Of course it helps if you know how a boot should fit. Most people don't. We wear casual shoes or dress shoes made of very pliable leather. We generally don't walk much in them. Boots are made for walking — be they hunting boots, hiking boots, or winter boots. Even waders are made for walking, although you'd never know it to walk in them. Therefore, I like that kind of wader that you wear with felt-soled wading shoes. I need all the help I can get in a trout stream.

Sizing a boot you'll be walking in is different than sizing a dress shoe. For one thing, you may be carrying a load on your back in the backcountry, even if you're not a regular backpacker. Even a ten-pound "possibles bag" puts an additional load on your feet and alters your posture, which in turn alters the way you walk. A heavier load of the sort you might backpack into a remote trout pond for a weekend puts a tremendous load on your feet and legs. If you're not accustomed to toting forty pounds on your back, it'll feel like a ton. Particularly if your boots don't fit!

All this implies that you should take your time selecting footgear for the outdoors. The first rule of thumb by which you must live is that no one pair of boots will do everything for you. In the same vein, no pair of boots fitted for summer and fall use will have enough room in them to add extra insulation and make them suitable for winter use. Let's differentiate right off the bat between the boots you'll wear in winter, and the boots you'll wear the rest of the year. Obviously, if you live in a place where there's no winter, you can forget about winter boots.

Winter or summer, though, they all fit the same.

I used to refuse to fit boots for a customer in my shop unless he or she either brought the heavy socks they'd be wearing with them, or bought socks from me to wear in the boots, and used them for try-ons. In terms of length and width, you can fit three whole sizes in less than a half an inch. This tells you that the socks you'll be wearing are a significant part of achieving a good fit. Bring socks with you, or get socks at your outfitter's. What you'll want is a pair of ragg wool socks with a thin liner sock, preferably wool, under them. If you're allergic to wool, a high-bulk synthetic like *Orlon,* with a synthetic liner sock, will work almost as well. These socks will protect your feet against blisters, cushion your feet as you walk, and transmit some, but not all, moisture to the air as you walk.

It helps, I suppose, if you know your shoe size, but I'd prefer to have my feet measured by a shoe fitting gizmo called a Brannock Device. Insist, if you must, that both feet be measured, because the odds are that one is larger than the other. Why the Brannock Device? Because it measures arch length as well as overall length. The arch length is the truly critical fit. For example, if your left foot measures an 11 in overall length and a 10½ in arch length, that 11 boot may not support your foot properly. On the other hand, you may not be able to fit a 10½ without driving your toes into the toe box of the boot with every step, particularly every downhill step. Sometimes you can, though. A good boot fitter can tell you which of the boots he has will accommodate your foot best. Some 10½'s may run just large enough that a compromise is possible. Others don't. That knowledge is why you go to this kind of shop in the first place!

An experienced boot fitter can almost look at the way a boot laces and tell you whether or not it fits. In the long run, *you* have to be the judge. Here's how to judge.

The boot has to fit you for overall length, arch length, heel width, instep girth, and ball girth. The best test for overall length is a simple one. Put the boot on, unlaced. Slide your foot forward until your toes just touch the toe box. Now, slide your index finger down the back of the boot, between the heel cup and your heel. You should be able to fit your index finger comfortably. Not sloppily, not forced; comfortably. That should give you plenty of clearance, and your toes shouldn't hit the toe box when you walk downhill. This should also allow your feet to "grow" as you walk with a heavy load.

Heel width is a little tougher to evaluate, because a new boot, be it a lightweight, knockabout field boot or a sturdy hiking boot of the sort you might wear on a high country hunt in Wyoming, will be stiff enough right off the bat that the heel will ride up a bit as you walk. However, if you slide your foot back into the heel cup without lacing the boot, and then walk a few steps, the boot should fit well enough around your heel that it doesn't drop off your foot, or even come close to it. In other words, there should be a gentle "cupping" action that cradles your heel and holds it in place.

There's such a thing as too much heel cup. A severely cupped heel may dig into your Achilles tendon and actually bruise it. Use your own judgment, and assume that, in time, most boots will mold somewhat to the configuration of your heel. Just remember that a boot which doesn't fit, or fits uncomfortably, will never ever break in. A boot that fits well will fit better as it grows old along with you, but no amount of breaking in will ever make a bad boot good.

Instep girth is relatively simple to check out, assuming your foot is somewhere in the "normal" ballpark. If it isn't, and you have an exceptionally high instep, you'll have a great problem getting certain types of boots to fit. The material to accommodate a large instep girth has to come from somewhere. Usually it comes from the ball girth of the boot. If you look at the conventional hiking boot with its long lacing system that extends nearly to the toe box, you can see that a boot of this design will more easily accommodate disparate instep girths than will a boot that begins its lacing at or near the maximum girth of the instep. In other words, you may have trouble fitting into high-topped hunting boots unless they lace to the toe.

How can you tell if the instep girth is okay? Easy. It'll hurt if it's too small. If, on the other hand, the boot is far too large, you wont' be able to lace it snugly.

Ball girth—the "width" most of us are concerned with—is easy to check out. Just remember this simple rule. Any pressure is too much pressure. The purpose of a boot is to protect your feet. Part of this protection comes from the fact that a boot gently restrains your feet into a compact, functional shape under load. "Gentle" is the key. Your feet will spread as you walk, and they'll spread even more under a heavy load like a pack. A boot that's snug in the store will be intolerable after a few miles of walking. Ideally, with the boot laced at normal lacing pressure, you should be able to draw up a little wrinkle of leather across the ball of your foot by pushing from both sides of the boot toward the center. Just a little one, mind you. If your bootseller has packs around—and he should, because bootsellers who don't frequently fail to comprehend the demands of backcountry walking with a pack—load one up and tromp around the shop for a few minutes. You'll learn pretty quickly whether the boot fits across the ball girth. And every place else!

Fitting a boot is one problem. Finding one that doesn't self-destruct is another. It's apt to be complicated by the fact that the glove-soft boot with a wimpy sole construction is very often the easiest boot to fit. Once you see how these boots are made, it's easy to see why they fit. There's no structure to maintain your foot form.

Some people simply assume that the soft, wimpy boot will fall apart in a year. They buy them and frequently throw them away. Me? I like the feel of a solidly-made pair of boots. I'm willing to take the time to find a pair that fits, and more than willing to maintain them so that they'll continue to be warm and dry and comfortable. Maintenance is a simple and pleasant ritual at the end of a day. Clean the mud off the boots, stuff them with newspapers if they're damp or wet, and place them in a warm place to dry slowly. Remove the newspapers the next day, treat the leather to a good wax-based waterproofing compound like *Sno-Seal, Bee Seal,* or *Snow Proof,* and put shoe trees in the boots. Easy. Sure, it takes time. So does tying bass bugs, or airing out your sleeping bag, or cleaning your shotgun. Just do it. Your feet will love you for it.

While tender, loving care can help keep a lousy boot dry for a while, and even increase its limited lifespan, it can never make up for its initial lack of quality.

The cheapest boots are those made with uppers that are simply glued in some form or other to the soles. Stuff in an insole, and kick it out the door. A glued sole, or a vulcanized sole, can be very waterproof. No stitches for water to leak through; no insole or midsole fastenings to worry about. But—no structure to protect your feet, and nothing at all to prevent the boot from simply unpeeling and failing catastrophically in the backcountry. Believe me, this is a poor way to end a day of pheasant hunting.

There are two relatively simple, effective ways to make decent boots at a decent price. One is the well-known Goodyear welt construction, and the other is the inside-stitchdown, or Littleway construction technique. At the high end, and usually reserved for heavy-duty mountain boots, is the Norwegian welt.

A lot of boots are sold as Goodyear welt boots that really aren't. A true Goodyear welt boot is a stitched boot. It may be glued, too, or vulcanized for a very waterproof seal, but it is still stitched. How is it made? The upper, which is already sewn, is rolled out at the bottom and stitched inward to the insole and downward, through a thin strip of leather (the welt) and through the midsole or midsoles. The outsole is then bonded to the midsole.

The Littleway boot (so called because the first machine made to do this kind of sewing was a Littleway; the actual machine used today may be a Littleway or a Blake or something else) is made by rolling the bottom of the uppers inward around the insole and stitching from the outside through the midsole, the uppers, and the insole.

The Norwegian welt looks a little bit like a Goodyear, except that the welt caps both the stitching that goes through the upper into the midsole and the double line of stitching that goes through the upper and midsole structure. Again, this method of construction is usually reserved for very heavy-duty boots, which generally have very limited uses in the field.

In general, all of these methods were developed for leather insoles and midsoles, although they're easily enough adapted to synthetic materials. But a boot is a lot more than just how the uppers are fastened to the sole structure, however important this may be in terms of waterproof qualities and durability. The uppers are of equal importance. To understand the uppers, we'd best take a quick look at leather.

Today, other substances are slipping into bootmaking; some of them are well received and long overdue. The part fabric upper offers

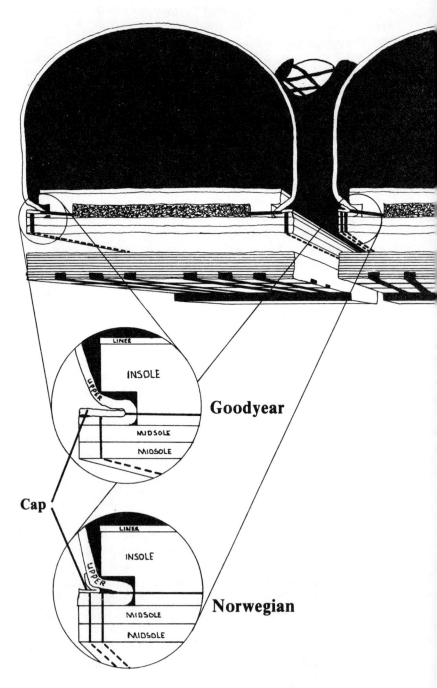

LINER

INSOLE

Goodyear

MIDSOLE

MIDSOLE

Cap

LINER

INSOLE

Norwegian

MIDSOLE

MIDSOLE

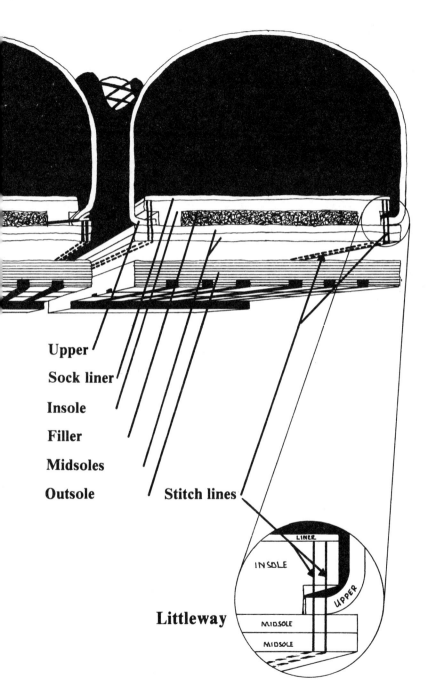

Upper

Sock liner

Insole

Filler

Midsoles

Outsole

Stitch lines

Littleway

LINER

INSOLE

UPPER

MIDSOLE

MIDSOLE

a considerable gain in breathability and a considerable reduction in weight. But even with these boots, the critical wear areas are still leather.

Most boot leather begins as cattle hide. A "hide", by the way, refers to the skin of a mature, large animal; a "skin" is from either a small animal or an immature animal. Thus, cowhide and horsehide as opposed to calfskin and goatskin. The conversion of Bessie's pelt into something fit for stalking through the corn fields of Nebraska hunting ringnecks is an involved process that begins with the removal of excess fats, hair and flesh, and ends (almost) with tanning, a chemical conversion of a very biodegradable hide into a more or less stable substance called leather.

In the old days leather was tanned with what are called "bark tannins", vegetable compounds that contained high amounts of tannic acid, the commonest of which was hemlock bark. Today most leather is chrome tanned, with soluble chromium salts as the tanning medium, although a lot of leather is combination tanned, with bark tannins and chromium. You see, when bark-tanned leather is wet, it dries as stiff as. . . well, as stiff as a boot! Chrome tanned leather is much softer after drying, but doesn't hold its shape as well. Hence the combination tanning process. Typically, leather is retanned after the initial combination bath, and some strange and wondrous substances are added. Silicones for water resistance, non-hydroscopic oils to exclude water and to add flexibility, waxes to exclude water — you name it.

After the leather is tanned, it is split, usually before the second tanning operation. Full hides, contrary to popular belief, are simply too thick for bootmaking. At this point, you can begin to see once of the three common types of leather used in bootmaking: full grain, roughout, and split. Full grain, or shell grain, leather, is leather with the hair removed but the natural surface of the skin remaining, complete with healed range scars and fly bites. The natural surface of the leather is the densest, the toughest, and the most inherently water-repellent. It is also that part of the leather that's most susceptible to abrasion damage. One way to protect the shell against abrasion is to turn it inside out. The resulting leather is called "roughout". It is most emphatically *NOT* suede, although it may have a sueded (brushed) finish. Suede is a thin brushed-nap leather made from a split, or the inside of the full hide.

A third type of leather is called split leather. It's what's left after the top grain has been skived away. With a looser fiber than the top grain, it will stretch more than the top grain and is essentially more porous. Split leather boots can range from very, very good to absolute junk, depending on the bootmaker. Some bootmakers "stuff" the leather with waxes and oils during a retanning, and back the split leather with a doubler to help it hold its form.

As far as leather goes, you can't always tell whether or not a boot is a split or a roughout by looking, although price is a pretty obvious giveaway. Not always, though. The best boots I own, made by an outfit renowned the world over for their mountaineering boots, are of split leather. As far as I can tell, it must have been from a tyrannosaurus or something. This stuff is heavy! And tough... And as absolutely waterproof as a boot can be. Unfortunately, if I had to replace these little gems, which I got some years back when I was doing a lot of mountaineering and some high-country hunting, I'd have to pony up somewhere around $215. At my age, I doubt if I warrant a pair of boots that good any more. But damn, they're comfortable! And those suckers fit! On second thought, maybe I would spend that kind of money on a pair of boots.

What may be more important in checking out a pair of boots is how the uppers are built. Too many seams are simply that many more entry points for water, and that many more things to fail. The best boots are basically one piece of leather, with tongues and such added. These things are added in such a way that water won't find little pockets to lie in.

When you look over a pair of boots, don't get wrapped up in the mystique of what they should look like. You know what I mean. There's this image of the Mighty Hunter in his twelve-inch lace-ups with moccasin toes that's hard to overcome. It's also a lot of weight to truck around for a day, even if you're hunting in snake country. Me? I use hiking boots most of the time, except in winter, when I switch to a true winter boot. Lately I've been wearing something that looks like a very heavy-duty running shoe for three-season roaming, and I find it excellent. I know I'll get teased about the silver gray color with the orange swoosh, but these little low-cuts have marvelous soles that provide a solid platform for walking, and nylon and leather uppers that are light and dry and comfortable. If it's reasonably dry, they're the boots I wear. If it's wet, I wear a pair of medium-weight hiking boots.

It's worth pointing out that many bootmakers are using what could be called running shoe technology today to make very light, very comfortable boots in all styles from Supersneakers to high-tops. Some are adapting the fabric uppers to the traditional heavy-duty sole structures. The results on these boots in terms of long-range durability aren't in, but the potential for dry, light, tough footgear is there. Even if it doesn't look traditional.

Winter's a different can of worms. If you're willing to live with wet feet, and carry a lot of socks, you can get by most of the year in the so-called Temperate Zone with sneakers, I suppose. But not in winter. Here, keeping warm and dry is more than a comfort and a convenience. It's a matter of life and death at its most extreme.

There are insulated leather boots around that are very waterproof. A lot of people like them for winter, and I find them plenty pleasant and comfortable myself. but somehow I don't feel that they're quite what I want when the weather gets severe, and I'm wandering around in rough country looking in vain for a whitetail, or freezing my butt out on a frozen lake, or sitting in the snow of a winter's evening calling fox.

At that point I want a boot made for severe winter use. Fortunately I have a few options. The first option is the ubiquitous insulated *shoepac,* the leather-topped, rubber-bottomed jobs that you see almost everywhere. At their best, well-sewn and with thick wool felt liners, they're excellent. The cheap ones tend to leak, though, which can cause major problems. If there's a drawback to these boots, it's that the liners can get wet if you step through thin ice when you're crossing a bog. However, if you're out in the backcountry for a full day's hunt, or even a walk without a pack, and that pack doesn't contain an extra pair of liners, you deserve what you get.

If the *shoepacs* aren't quite warm enough on the bitterest days, you can augment their insulation by adding an insole of closed-cell foam underneath the felt liner. I like *Ensolite* for that, and a quarter-inch thick *Ensolite* insole is both comfortable and remarkably warm. I also use it to pad out the seat on my racing canoes. Those seats are comfortable by themselves, but if you're as slatty as I am, a seventy mile canoe race gets a bit long!

The other option for severe weather is the U.S. Army boots known variously as Korea boots or Mickey Mouse boots. These are double wall boots with an insulation layer, usually foam, sealed against moisture between the walls. The insulation extends around the foot and well up to mid-calf. While these monsters aren't the pinnacle of lightweight technology, the black K-boots will keep you cozy at about -25° F if you're sitting on your duff doing nothing, and the white ones are probably warm to -60° F. Needless to add, you don't need socks with these boots, except to absorb perspiration, of which there'll be plenty. For that purpose, thick cotton socks will work as well as anything.

Please, though, whatever you do, don't try to make your summer boots into winter boots by simply trying to cram another pair of socks or two into them. All you'll do is cut off circulation to your feet. You'd be far, far better off to find a huge old pair of five buckle Arctic overshoes, slip in a huge felt *shoepac* liner, and wear your regular boots inside that arrangement. It'll keep you warm and dry. And for not much money.

Chapter 9
Hats, Gloves and Mittens

Headgear is so important in cold weather that it warrants a separate chapter. The old North Country adage, "When your feet are cold, put your hat on", is more than a truism. It's based on rock-solid physiology.

If you'll hearken back to our talks about insulation and about the physiology of cold, you'll remember that our bodies don't throttle down the flow of warm, oxygen-rich blood to our heads and torsos. In time, the blood supply to the head throttles down to a point where you become irrational and want to go to sleep. That point's well into severe hypothermia, and you're in grave trouble. Meanwhile, in normal situations, about fifteen percent of your heat gets blown out through your scalp and the nape of your neck. In cold weather, when you're beginning to do little dances to keep warm, that figure may approach thirty percent. That's a lot of heat to lose.

This certainly means that your head must be well protected. There are times in cold weather when you may choose to go bareheaded, but this is only when you're working hard and want to blow off some heat to keep from building up too much sweat in your insulation. This doesn't mean that you ever go out in cold weather without headgear. It also means that, to preserve your options and to keep your powder dry, you need headgear that is sufficiently flexible to permit gradations in ventilation—even if it means carrying two hats.

Come to think of it, that's not a bad idea. I do it all the time.

Hats should be wool, although bulky Orlon is acceptable. Some folks can't stand the feel of wool on their hides, and Orlon is a decent substitute.

The hat is not the traditional red-checked or orange cap of the hunter, with cute little earlappers that never quite go over your ears. It's a woolen Balaclava, something developed by the British army in the Crimean War to keep the troops warm. Like most things British, it appears strange to the untutored eye, but it works.

Basically, it resembles a Navy pea hat or watch cap with a long tail that you can pull down to your collarbone if lousy weather demands it. Obviously there's a neat little hole for your eyes, nose and mouth. This "skirt" folds up to be a three-layer earmuff around your temples, over your ears, and across the back of your neck if you wish, or you can fold it one notch higher and expose your ears. Some Balaclavas even have neat little knitted bills that don't do much, but they will keep snow from falling down behind your glasses.

A neat hat, believe me. Loosely knitted; so in a high wind you may need additional protection against wind losses. But at that point, you're probably not hunting anyway, so you may as well put up your parka hood.

Hats get wet from sweat and snow, despite our best intentions. While a damp wool hat may be better than no hat at all, it isn't much better. And it's no problem at all to stow an extra wool hat in your pack or your pocket for such instances, or to wear just while you're walking. This is my preferred approach. A watch cap, or a lightweight Norwegian ski hat (complete with tassel) that's long enough to cover the nape of my neck if I need, is my walking hat, and that goes into a pocket or into a pack when it's time to stop or slow down. Then the trusty Balaclava comes out. I've never seen a Norwegian wool hat in blaze orange, but I've seen a lot of them in a very clear, bright red. and the Balaclava, which is a favorite of mountaineers and ice climbers, is usually available in orange. It's not a true international orange, but it surely doesn't look like the southern part of a northbound whitetail, either.

Hats for the rest of the year? Take your pick. I like a wide-brimmed fisherman's hat for rain protection—the classic sou'wester you see in the old lithographs. They work. When I'm out in the sun, I'm a great fan of a strange little hat made by Columbia, called the *Up-Downer*. It's kind of a combination of crusher hat and long-billed sportfisherman's cap—which is to say that there's a long peak in front and a narrow brim around the rest of the cap that you can turn up or down as you need. You can also turn it bass-ackwards if there's a bright sun at your back, and keep your neck from roasting. It's the greatest fishing cap, canoe tripping cap, and bird hunting cap in the known universe.

I also like wide-brimmed tropical weight porkpie hats with wide brims and chin straps, even though I feel like I'm ready to jump into a small boat in South Florida and go unseat El Presidente, whoever he may be. The hats are comfortable. And I like the classic Jones Hat for beating through the bush, as long as it isn't foam-lined or tricked out with ridiculous earlappers that don't cover your ears but do cover your forehead.

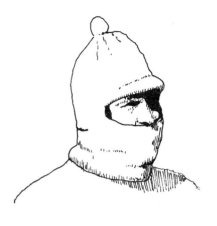

Balaclava

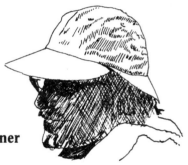

The irreplaceable Up-Downer

Basic wool cap

101

If this sounds like I have a beef against some clothing designers, you're right. A hat is a fairly simple item to build, and not complex to design. Yet, the typical hook and bullet shop is stocked with hats that are an insult to the intelligence of a three-toed sloth. Bad materials, gimmicky designs, no comprehension of what a hat has to do—you wonder if these dudes have ever had their bootsoles on anything but pavement or carpet! Hell's bells, man, a half day at the beach ought to teach you enough to do better headgear than you usually find.

Keeping your hands warm can be major problem. If you're just poking around on a cold day, enjoying the snow and the scenery, it's easy. Heavy mittens abound. Army surplus woolen mittens with insulated or uninsulated overshells are available if you're lucky. Most cross-country ski shops and backpacking shops carry heavy ragg wool mittens or felted wool mittens and overshells to keep your mittens dry and reduce wind penetration. You can even find down or synthetic-filled expedition mittens.

All these things will keep your hands warm, but most of them are useless for field sports, because your dexterity is impaired. However, there are things you can do. The duck hunter, who's usually out in miserable weather, has some warning when a shot is coming up. He can wear monster mitts and slip out of them before he shoots. The deer hunter on a stand has the same option. The still hunter for deer doesn't; neither does the rabbit hunter. There are mitten shells made with trigger fingers, though, and if you're wearing woolen gloves under them, you can poke a finger up into the trigger finger shell and do the job. For chilly, but not bitter, weather, there are fingerless woolen gloves available. For cold weather fishing, the fingerless wool gloves are hard to beat. Sure, your fingertips will get cold, but that's far preferable to having the whole hand feel like a block of ice up to the elbow.

You can't do much if your hands are wet and cold. In the long run, you'll do better and feel better in the field if your hands are warm—even if it means wriggling one hand out of a heavy mitten to shoot—than you will if you freeze in the approved manner.

For the record, vapor barrier gloves (surgeon's gloves or hairdresser's gloves) can be very effective under a wool glove. Try it. And whatever handwarming solution you arrive at, I suggest you try using it for shooting on a practice range. I know. Shooting in heavy mittens in August will certainly set your buddies to howling. Remind them of it when you drop your deer and they miss because their hands were cold, or they had trouble finding the safety with mittens on.

Sometimes the obvious is overlooked. Commercial pocket

handwarmers can certainly provide added comfort. Just make sure you have enough fuel to get them started and keep them going. An external heat source will certainly warm up those cold hands in a pit or stand as well. Just don't set yourself (or anything else) on fire. And don't miss that twelve pointer or let that easy double whiz by while you're paying more attention to warming up.

Chapter 10

Food and Water

Part of keeping warm and dry is clothing; part of keeping warm and dry is good judgement and proper body management; part of keeping warm and dry is maintaining enough fuel for your metabolic fires, and enough water to keep you from getting dehydrated.

Food is a bit of a luxury in the summer. You won't die of hunger in a boat if you forgot your sandwiches. But you can be in very serious trouble on a hot day if you forget your drinking water. It's nice to think that all you have to do is dip down and drink, but the places where you can do this have become regrettably few in the United States. Even if industrial waste hasn't fouled the water, there's a good chance that some natural bug that does strange and wondrous things to your digestive tract has.

In cold weather, when you're blowing out a lot of calories just to keep warm, food becomes more of a necessity. It's not that most of us couldn't stand to lose a few pounds or more. But losing them on a day's hunt is a poor place to do it. It takes time to teach your body to reach down and tap your fat supply for food. Dieters can do it in time; trained distance athletes do it routinely. there's no way you can store enough glycogen to run a marathon, and no way you could eat on the run to maintain a supply in your blood. You tap the free lipids in your system.

But you're not going to do that on a hunting trip. You'll take food with you—and a few other things. You'll also take water with you, or you'll have a good enough knowledge of the country you hunt to know where there's water available. And you'll drink before you're thirsty and eat before you're hungry if you want to stay warm and be comfortable, cheerful and alert in the woods. Cold weather is insidious. You don't feel thirsty, generally, and you rarely sweat heavily. But you lose a huge amount of fluids simply by warming the cold air that you inhale. Before you know it, you're dehydrated and easy meat for hypothermia and frostbite. You're also easy meat for what's generally referred to as "altitude sickness". This shouldn't bother most of us, but anybody who gets a chance to hunt in the high country of the Rockies should keep this in mind. If you're a high country resident, you've had the benefit of some acclimatization to elevations, but it's rough enough on a flatlander from Illinois for a few days without helping it along by dehydration.

I dramatize some of the effects of dehydration a bit, I suppose. Most times, you just won't feel as sharp as you should, and you'll get chilly easier. You won't wind up hypothermic, and have to be evacuated by a National Guard chopper from Elk Lake in a snowstorm. But just feeling flatter than usual and chilly around the edges is bad enough.

There you are. You've worked forty-nine weeks, and you take a two-week vacation in summer. You save one week for a deer hunt. Now you and I both know that it's nice to get a deer, but you'd go hunting even if somebody gave you a written guarantee that you wouldn't get so much as a glance at a doe vanishing in the distance. In the long run, hunting is the least important part of hunting.

But this year you've arranged to go into the Wyoming high country for elk with some old friends. It cost you a bundle, to be sure—but any vacation costs you a bundle. It costs you 48 to 50 weeks of work. Don't forget that. The dollars are secondary to that one screaming fact. You have worked twenty-five hours for every hour you have on this vacation. To have less than a great time and wonderful memories because you let yourself get dehydrated is unthinkable. To miss a once-in-a-lifetime shot because you were chilly and your stomach was sour from hunger pangs is worse.

Yet, we've all done it. I have; I know. Countless times. But I'm getting too old for that. There aren't as many hunts and fishing trips and canoe trips and hikes left for a forty-seven year old. And I can't waste one of them by being dumb. Now this doesn't mean I plan to go out there swathed in a vacuum bottle, with a bevy of medical people at my side. It doesn't for damn sure mean that I'll portage any more rapids than I do now, either. I'll take the same risks I've always taken, because I suppose, at the end, I'd rather be a dead lion than a live mouse. Meanwhile, I refuse to be dumb and have the good times diminished because I'm cold, wet, hungry or thirsty. That's not roughing it. That's not playing the game. That's being a damn fool.

Hikers regularly carry polybottles of water and trail munchies of some sort, if not lunches. Even if water is generally available, they'll carry a water bottle, because the time to drink is when you're thirsty.

For some outdoor activities like stream fishing or bird hunting, you're generally close enough to the car to leave a bottle of water there and drink hearty when you return for lunch. Or you can take a pint of water with you. With all the junk I take trout fishing, I'd have to look through ten pockets to find a pint of water!

If you're fishing from a boat, you can live like a member of the royal family. I fish a lot from canoes, and even in my little racing solo boat—a neat fishing boat, by the way—there's room enough for a small cooler and some food and water. I never was one for knocking down beer on a fishing trip. After the day is over? Sure. During the day? No, thanks.

The only times food and water become a real consideration is on an extended hunt, particularly in cool or cold weather. Deer hunting and running hounds for 'coon come to mind immediately. Duck hunting is generally done in the foulest weather imaginable, but you can set up housekeeping in a blind if you have to, right down to the small gasoline stove. But deer and 'coon demand walking. And long times afield.

The wise hunter carries a pack. Not a monster designed for overnighting. Just a so-called daypack. You might as well get a good one while you're at it. The good ones will run you a twenty dollar bill more than the cheap ones, but you'll easily see the difference. Into that pack you should stuff some food, water, and maybe even a small stove and one pot to brew up a pot of tea in the dull time around noon. Or maybe some soup. Who knows. Believe me, once you get in the habit of doing it, you'll wonder why you didn't do it year ago.

You might even want to treat yourself to a hot meal out there, right on the stump you've been sitting on. It's easy. Whip out the little stove, fire it up, stew up some water, and use that hot water to either heat up a gourmet meal in a bag like beef burgundy, or stir it into a precooked, freeze dried *Mountain House* meal. What's your fancy? Shrimp Creole? Lasagna? Turkey Tetrazzini? They're all available. And they're not too shabby. Even the franks and beans are good. Drowse in the sun for a half hour, fire up the stove and have another cup of coffee or tea, eat a candy bar or some dry fruit, and you're ready for another half day of hunting with a smile on your face.

Clue your hunting partners in on this. You tote the stove, and your own food (in case you should fail to rendezvous for some reason), and have them over to your stump for dinner. It's a pleasant way to talk about the morning's hunt, and to make plans for the afternoon. It'll keep them happier and more alert too.

Now, you don't need a chef and his *batterie de cuisine* to do this. You need one pot that will hold maybe a quart and half of water, a pot lifter, an insulated plastic cup, a tablespoon, and a small stove. I prefer a gas stove to the LP or butane stoves. The latter are simpler and quicker to use, but the gasoline unit really gets the steam up in a hurry. What do I prefer? For this kind of use, the Coleman *Peak I,* the Svea *123,* and the Enders *Benzin Baby.* The Coleman is the heaviest of the bunch, but the simplest to use. The Svea is light, compact and utterly reliable, but a little less stable than the Coleman. The Enders is a little blowtorch, but it has to be assembled in the field (no great task) and it's not a stove you can find everywhere. The NATO troops use it, and the *Wehrmacht* used one very like it in the war. It works.

You don't need to carry spare fuel for the little brutes, although you can find 250cc fuel flasks in some shops that are just the ticket for day trips and overnight trips, where most of the larger fuel bottles would be a pain in the rear to tote.

Come to think of it, there's nothing to prevent you from doing this on any trip. Heck, you can fry up some of the morning's catch on the bow seat of the boat, if you want to. Why not? It sure beats American cheese and bologna on what passes for white bread, doesn't it?

The process is hardly more complex for a weekend of trout fishing up at the headwaters of some stream. Freeze-dried food abounds in all backpacking shops, and there's a generous selection of easy-to-make one pot meals at the local supermarket. You don't have to live on canned hash, pork and beans, and Dinty Moore Beef Stew if you don't want to.

The only problem is water. For cooking, it's less of a problem. Boiling for fifteen minutes will kill just about anything, and iodine tablets or chlorine-liberating tablets like *Halazone* will be effective for almost any problem that could be caused by water in the backcountry.

A little bit of local knowledge doesn't hurt, either. Hunting over strange country can be remarkably unproductive. But hunting country that you've hiked over on a few weekends in the summer with your family can be money in the bank. While you're doing this, you can probably scout out a few sources of water. This is handy for you. It means you won't have to carry as much with you in the fall. And, if you hadn't noticed, deer like to drink, too. Find water and sooner or later you'll find deer — and just about everything else as well.

Besides, it's fun. And that's what being outdoors is all about.

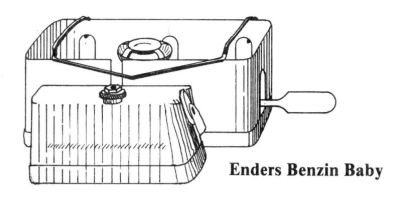

Enders Benzin Baby

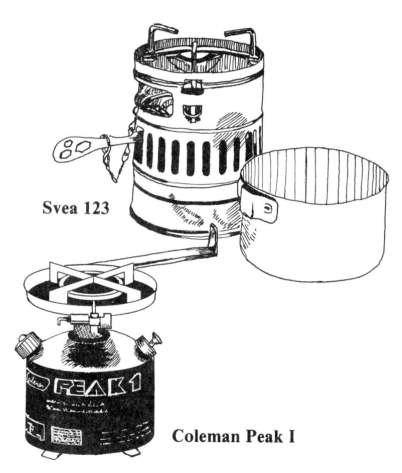

Svea 123

Coleman Peak I

Chapter 11

Being Prepared:
Your Favorite Outdoor Activities

You know, you can talk all you want about theory and technical considerations, and all that jazz. When you finish, somebody will always ask, "Hey, this is fine, but what do you wear when you go...?" Here are some answers.

I'd like to tell you what I'd wear while doing a lot of different activities. Let's assume we've got all the money we need, but we don't necessarily want the most expensive items. I'm choosing the things that would work best for me. At the end of this long ramble, you'll find that the list can be consolidated, trimmed down, and weeded out to a few broadly useful, practical garments that will cover a lot of situations.

It's a temptation to name names, but unless an item is unique, I'll refrain. Again, what suits me may not suit you. Since you're the one who wants to keep warm and dry, try to make some mental adjustments between my frame and situation, and yours.

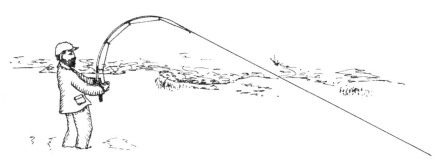

Fishing: Shore, Wading, and Boat

A lot of times you're close enough to the car that you don't have to carry much of anything with you for rain or wind. In cold weather, I like wool pants over polypropylene underwear, and a wool shirt over poly. I wear a fishing vest even in a boat. Because I'm a fly fisherman and a superlight spinning fisherman, I don't need too much in the way of large tackle boxes. A little *Plano* Mini-Magnum box holds all the small Dardevles and Little Cleos I need for the spinning rod. A couple of small fly boxes do me the rest of the time. If it's windy or the weather looks like rain is on the way, I'll stow a lightweight nylon rain jacket in the back of the vest if I'm wading. If I'm in a boat, I'll take a rain jacket and rain pants of a heavier sort. What I prefer is the sort of raingear commercial fishermen and heavy-duty blue water sailors wear, and what I use is Peter Storm PVC coat raingear. That's a jacket and bib-top pants. Bombproof. I'll also wear a hat. If it's cold out, I'll wear a watch cap. If it's just moderately nasty, I'll wear that silly-looking Columbia *Up-Downer.*

In warm weather, I'll still go with the heavy-duty raingear if I'm away from the car, otherwise I'll tote the lightweight jacket. I dispense with the wool and the poly and go to plain old Jockey undershorts and a net undershirt, with tan shirts and trousers from the local work clothing shop to keep the sun off. I wear my mesh *Up-Downer,* and I keep a pile jacket in the car if it's chilly when I return.

No dream stuff here. And not much need for dream stuff. Waders are terrible, but until the rivers are warm enough to wade in old sneakers or felt-soled sneakers and shorts, you have to live with them.

Fishing, Ice

What I'd prefer to wear if I had access to any gear in the world would be just about what I wear now. I was lucky to have accumulated some heavy-duty expedition gear in the past, and it does the job. From the inside out, poly underwear, top and bottom. Lightweight is fine. Pile shirt or wool shirt, wool pants, Balaclava, goose down expedition parka, lightweight socks, and white Mickey Mouse boots. If it's really windy, I'll put on a pair of nylon windpants, but it has to be howling for that to happen. I wear G.I. surplus heavy-duty insulated mittens with rayon contact gloves underneath for doing things like baiting hooks. And I take off the parka and unzip the pile shirt or unbutton the wool shirt whenever I'm in the shanty. Even in an unheated shelter, it's rarely necessary to zip up the parka. I always carry sunglasses if I'm on water or snow. The difference in comfort is amazing.

Hunting, Birds and Bunnies (Fall)

The key elements here are comfort for walking, and, if you choose and the hunting laws permit, a degree of camouflage. I'm not sure that either the birds or the bunnies care a damn, but I feel better if I'm dressed in unobtrusive clothing. And if I feel better, I shoot better.

While fall hunts can be cool, or even chilly, generally you're dealing with warm weather. I wear my "uniform" — tan work shirt and trousers — with lightweight hiking boots, a Jones hat and an old canvas field coat. Given my druthers, I'd like a spiffy shirt in heavy cotton from Patagonia or Robbins, tan Canoe Specialist trousers made of a fabric that stretches a bit when you walk, and a *Gore-Tex* parka, in camouflage and uninsulated. I'd probably treat myself to a *Gore-Tex* crusher hat in camouflage as well. I could use the *Gore-Tex* pants to match the parka, but I suspect that if the rain came down hard, I'd pack it in and go back to the house or car. I don't hunt over a dog at present, and it's tough kicking out birds or bunnies in a rain. However, I could use the *Gore-Tex* pants for other things, too, so as long as I'm dreaming, I may as well dream hard.

Hunting: Waterfowl

Why is it that some of the most uncongenial-seeming activities are among the most pleasant? In my neck of the woods (Upstate New

York) duck hunting and whitewater canoeing take place in miserable weather. Yet I can't think of two activities that are much more pleasureable. I could also add steelhead fishing to the list.

Duck hunting is basically sedentary, once you've gotten everything set up. You freeze in the pre-dawn mists and congeal in the post-dawn wind-driven rain. You need insulation, because you're out in bad weather, and you need very good rain protection because there's nowhere to hide, and it's always raining. Yet, you're active enough that you can work up a heavy sweat getting there and getting your blocks out.

Here's a place for the full synthetic outfit. Poly underwear, fiberpile jacket, fiberpile or bunting "pants", and a *Gore-Tex* or *Klimate* parka and pants. An insulated *Gore-Tex* hat would be a nifty touch, as would fingerless wool gloves. hands are a problem to keep warm, but you usually have the option of keeping your hands toasty in your parka pockets because you're not jump shooting. Even if you are, you generally know that there are birds up ahead, and you have some time to get ready. The duck blind is one place where a handwarmer is more than a luxury.

You may find that an insulated parka is more to your liking, and more versatile for your needs. If so, I'd go for a *Gore-Tex* or *Klimate* parka insulated with one of the thin, boundary layer fills like *Thinsulate* or *Sontique*. I'd pick a parka that had a reasonably simple front, because I don't like geegaws hanging up on gun butts, bows, or fly lines.

Footgear? Sometimes you're stuck with hip boots, and there's no choice. If this is the case, dedicate one pair of hip boots to duck hunting, and buy them roomy enough to accommodate the felt liners that come with winter shoepacs. In fact, with a little ingenuity, you can create felt or *Ensolite* closed-cell foam liners for your hip boots that will be marvelously comfortable for early-season trout and river smallmouth.

If you regularly hunt an area where you don't need boots like I do, shoepacs will work acceptably. However, I'd really like a pair of the new insulated *Gore-Tex* hunting boots that Danner makes. They're light, dry and warm. You can't ask for more than that.

There's one kind of migratory bird hunting I've never tried, and that's hunting goose from a pit, prairie style. The clothing I've seen that's been designed especially for it is interesting; three-quarter length insulated parkas and such. I can picture the requirements as being similar to the East Coast duck hunter's, except it may be a little drier and, if such is possible, a little colder.

Hunting: Big Game

This covers a lot of ground, and a tremendous temperature range. Southern deer hunters can survive nicely with a camouflaged mesh jacket and pants over as near to nothing as you can get away with, or as near to nothing as the mosquitos let you get away with. On the other hand, a deer hunt in Michigan's Upper Peninsula is subarctic hunting. There's also a world of difference in the clothing requirements of a bowhunter in a tree stand and a still hunter on the ground.

Some generalizations can be made. Let's start with bowhunting first. While some bowhunters stalk, most shoot from stands or blinds. The immobile hunter is frequently the cold hunter, as a quick look back to the Army insulation tables will remind you. It takes a lot less insulation to keep you warm when you're moving.

On the other hand, the hunter working from a blind has a few advantages. To begin with, it's easy to optimize your insulation if you don't have to worry about excessive perspiration. And to finish it off, while you may have to carry some gear back to the stand in a pack, you don't have to carry it once you're there. You can live like a king.

Bowhunting from a tree stand or blind seems to be the perfect spot for the breathable and waterproof qualities of the PTFE parkas and pants, with varied insulation underneath to suit the weather. The PTFE clothing (again, *Gore-Tex* or *Klimate*) can be worn almost by itself in warm weather, and over pile or wool or down in cold. It turns rain, ventilates well, and can be purchased in a great variety of fabrics, including some very quiet nylon, dacron and cotton blends. Fortunately these ideal fabrics are also available in camouflage. One manufacturer, Columbia, offers a wide range of such gear in in both tan and green camouflage, in *Gore-Tex, Klimate* and *Thinsulate,* coated heavy-duty nylon, and synthetic blend fabrics insulated with *Thinsulate.* It's an awesome array of very high-ticket outdoor gear.

Consider this for versatility, though. Even in the Frozen North of upstate New York, Maine, and Michigan's Upper Peninsula, bowhunting season can vary from Indian summer to very brisk indeed. Yet, you can plan a clothing array that looks like this: undershorts, net undershirt, lightweight poly tops and bottoms, pile jacket and pants, or bunting pants if you find them more comfortable, and a *Gore-Tex* parka and overpants. Warm day? Wear the parka and pants over the undershorts and string shirt. Cooler? Add the poly long john set—or add just the bottoms or tops, depending on what's cold. Generally, I add the bottoms first. Really cold? You still have the fiberpile jacket/shirt and the fiberpile or bunting pants to put on. If you think it'll be really bitter, put on a pile vest under the pile jacket, or put on a down or synthetic vest over the pile jacket. That much insulation—breathable insulation—under a parka and pants that can turn rain and still breathe, is very warm indeed. And dry, from the outside in and from the inside out.

If wool's your thing, use wool instead of the fiberpile. And whatever way you choose to go, bring some food in your pack, and some water. You'll be warmer, more comfortable and more alert.

The more traditional concept of deer hunting is that of cold-weather hunting, either by still hunting or driving. Here you have three different clothing problems to solve. The still hunter is moving, slowly and steadily, with a lot of stopping and looking. In fact, as I grow older, I find myself doing a lot of standing and looking, particularly when I'm going up hills. I tell my friends that it's so I can check on deer contouring around the slope, or to manage my body so I don't sweat as much. You and I know better.

The guy who draws the drive is moving, often briskly, and frequently with little care to find the easy route. He'll work up a sweat in spite of all precautions, unless he drives with very little clothing. So he has to dress lightly, and take a pack to tote the clothing he'll need when it's his turn on watch.

The guy on the stand is like the bowhunter. he's not doing much moving. The main difference is that he's usually parked his butt on the cold, cold ground. Of course, he's probably had some hard truckin' to get to the stand in the first place.

If this begins to sound like a put-it-on — take-it-off — put-it-on drill, you're beginning to get the message.

Unless the weather is better, or there's snow on the ground, choose lightweight footgear. It makes the walking easier—a whole lot easier. If you're walking through bog meadows, you may have to change your game plan somewhat, but keep the footgear light if you plan a lot of walking. You can always add a little warmth by pulling an outsized felt boot liner on over your boots when you're on watch.

They don't hold up for much walking, but they sure do the job in this application!

I'd wear a hard-weave wool for pants, and I'd be inclined to wear suspenders, because it's easier to ventilate the pants if they're loose around the middle. I can always cut down on heat loss with my parka if I need all the warmth I can get. And I'd wear lightweight polypropylene underwear, at least on the bottom. I'd carry overpants of *Gore-Tex* or *Klimate,* in case it snowed, rained, or I was on watch and needed the extra warmth. For underwear, I'd start with a heavyweight polypropylene undershirt with a couple of buttons at the neck. The one I wear is called the Wallace Beery Shirt, and it's made by SXC Polypro. Patagonia also makes a Wallace Beery shirt in heavyweight polypropylene. The buttons are essential for ventilation with the heavyweight polypropylene. The stuff is warm! On a mild winter day, you can walk with nothing on your upper body but one of these shirts—and I'll bet you you'll have the buttons unfastened.

Over that, I'd wear fiberpile—a full zip jacket rather than a half-zip pullover. Over that, I'd wear a PTFE parka. If it was a cold day, I'd be tempted to stow the parka in my pack and wear an inuslated parka over the pile and the poly undershirt. That's a lot to tote in a pack in terms of bulk, but the weight is insignificant. If the bulk bothers you, choose a space-filler insulation like down, *PolarGuard,* or *Hollofil II* with a light nylon shell. this will compress better in a pack. Or you can tote a down vest with a lightweight nylon shell as an extra garment. It weighs next to nothing and stuffs down to about the size of a Chicago softball.

I'd wear wool fingerless gloves, and I'd wear them under mittens or G.I. trigger finger mitten shells if it was cold, and I'd no more go out for a long hunt in tough country without extra socks and mittens, and an extra liner set for my boots, than I would go without my rifle. I'd wear my watch cap or my Balaclava, depending on the weather, and I'd certainly wear gaiters if it was snowy or if I had to roam around through marshes.

Out in the high country, where the distances you may cover are longer and the elevation is higher, I'd pay close attention to my boots. That's where the energy saving comes in. The old hiker's saw about a pound on your feet equalling five pounds on your back is never so apparent as when you're trucking around some very steep hillsides at over eight thousand feet elevation.

At any rate, high country or low country, if it's cold weather, I'd go prepared to add clothing and subtract it as needed, depending on what I was doing. If I have to hustle through the puckerbrush on a drive, even in very cold weather, I'll be warm with my parka and a heavyweight polypropylene undershirt and my watch cap. But when it's my turn to sit, I'll need the extras—the overpants, the pile jacket, maybe even the big insulated parka. And certainly the Balaclava, the heavy mitts, and the felt booties. To be cold on a stand is to miss shots on a stand. To be hungry and dehydrated is to miss shots, too. If you can keep from being cold, hungry and thirsty on a hunt by the simple procedure of carrying a small pack with extra clothing, and wearing versatile clothing, it sure seems smart to do it.

You'll notice that there's a pattern emerging here. For warm weather the words are light, dry and versatile. For cold weather, the words are warm, dry and versatile. All the gear I've chosen for active wear has a couple of things in common: it's breathable, doesn't absorb moisture, and it's reasonably lightweight. There's something else too, that I hadn't really thought of when I began making notes for this chapter. With the exception of wool pants and wool shirts, which I've considered mostly as alternates to fiberpile pants and jackets, there's nothing that's really "traditional". Further, there's hardly an item here that you can find at the average hook-and-bullet shop, unless it's a shop that also carries a lot of hiking and mountaineering equipment.

Time for another sermon. I suspect that one of the main reasons that most hook-and-bullet shops don't carry really functional outdoor clothing is that we've let a rift build up between the backpackers on one hand and the hunters and fishermen on the other hand. Me? I stand somewhere in the middle. I've hunted and fished since I was a kid, but I've also spent years in what I suppose could be called the ecology sports trade. I'm fed up to the eyeteeth with this schism. I'm not a blood-crazed killer because I hunt, as some of the extreme ecosport folks would label me. Neither am I a Commie-pinko-environmentalist-fag-hiker as some of the arch gun-toters and a few Department of Interior people might style me. I don't like labels. I particularly don't like labels when they come from some nut who's empowered to watch over public lands in my name. But that's neither here nor there. The gun shop people have been taught by all this nonsense to be wary of any person who's a sales rep for backpacking gear, and the backpacking rep has ben taught that he might get strung up by the local vigilantes if he takes his gear into a hook-and-bullet shop.

This works both ways. Camouflage gear in a backpacking shop? In some areas, like the Rockies and the South, you'll find it. In other areas, you won't. Same reasons. The guy repping the quality stuff that's available in camouflage has been taught that he'll get stomped by some feisty little old lady birdwatchers if he walks into a backpacking shop, and the dude running the shop has been taught to think that the hunting clothing huckster is probably carrying an Uzi and has a very fast trigger finger if he thinks you don't like snowmobiles.

This is fine for me. Because neither group talks to the other, and I work in both, I can write a book that tells one group that the other guys have some superb gear that they should know about. But I'd rather not have to do it under these conditions.

And you know who loses? You. Me. And everybody else who enjoys being outdoors, be they hikers or hunters. If you keep the users of the backcountry fighting each other, the folks who want to grind it to powder face no concerted opposition. The local politicians want to build a dam on a river because a few of them own land bought cheap that will be waterfront property when the impoundment fills up. The first thing that happens is that the fishermen and the canoeists start fighting each other. Why? Hell, they've always been fighting. Damn canoeists louse up the fishing! Damn fishermen think they own the river! Meanwhile the prime river users won't talk to each other. The pols bleat to the public about jobs and recreation, as if river fishing and paddling weren't. Both the fishermen and the paddlers wind up with another stagnant water skier's paradise that grows a great crop of carp. Smart! I don't know what you call it, but the tough-minded old Polish farmer I bought our farmhouse from would call it "pissing in the soup".

This isn't to gloss over the fact that the ecosport folks and the field sport folks have differences of opinion. But I'll tell you something. You, as a hunter, have more in common with the non-hunting birdwatcher than you do with the developer and the despoiler. You and the birdwatcher are using wild country for your recreation. Spell that in the old way — for your re-creation. Both of you turn to the wild country to re-create you in the middle of a high-pressure, artificial workaday world. You need each other. You don't have to agree, but you both have to understand each other's position, and regard it as honest.

Maybe it wouldn't change much, but you wouldn't feel foolish carrying a bird guide with you just to learn what's there, and the birdwatcher might discover that you can see more birds in camouflage clothing. That's a start.

Trapping

Trapping is right up there with duck hunting and ice fishing as far as potential discomfort levels go. In the good weather, it's no problem, except that in water season you're encumbered by boots or waders, even if you set mostly from a canoe. In cold weather you have to be ready for anything, because if you set them today, you'd best check them tomorrow, regardless of what tomorrow's weather brings. I wear what I'd wear for hunting in similar weather, and dress lightly rather than heavily because I'd be moving. Sure, it takes time to make a set properly, but not that much time if you've thought it out at home beforehand. And you can always stow a down vest in your pack basket, or even in the pocket of your parka. If you're working water sets from a canoe, you can use the heavy-duty raingear that makes you look like a North Sea fisherman, because you won't be working up quite the sweat that you would if you were trying to cover thirty-two dirt holes for fox on a chain of hills before you have to go home, shave and shower, and put on a business suit. Don't laugh. I know people who do just that.

In other words, poly underwear, wool or fliberpile pants and shirt, PTFE parka, or heavy-duty insulated parka, and maybe a down or pile vest in reserve if it's bitter cold. Heavy-duty raingear if it's bucketing out, or if you're not walking as much. And the usual extras like spare mittens. I've mentioned the frostbite I suffered on a trapline when I was twelve, when I got my mitts soaked on the only day of the season that I'd forgotten spares.

The upshot of that was one very, very sensitive left thumb, and spare mittens in every pocket. Yes, I tie my monster mitts to each other with nylon tape, and run the tape through the sleeves of my parka, in very cold weather. I like winter hiking, but it's no time to lose protection for a very vital part of your body. Think of it this way. You can walk out from the boondocks with badly frostbitten feet if you had to bivouac overnight due to weather conditions or injury. But you can't even unsnap a snap on your parka, or open a candy bar, with frostbitten hands. Neither option is exactly what the war-gamers would call viable, but if you keep that in mind, you'll learn to keep a careful watch on your mittens.

120

Canoeing

There's a difference between using a canoe as a platform for some other activity, like hunting, fishing or trapping, and using a canoe to go somewhere in. I do both. I also race, both whitewater and flatwater. Racing is a different bag. You wear as little as you can because of the heat build-up, but in whitewater, you must, by both racing rules and good sense, wear a life jacket, and in cold water a wet suit just may save your life if you dump the boat in a spot where you can't get out of the river quickly.

Canoeing, when you're using the boat to go somewhere, can be a very vigorous activity. I tend to paddle hard even when I'm tripping, because I like to paddle hard. So does my wife and so do my kids. But this is one of the few sports in which I eschew breathable rainwear, and go to the heavy-duty stuff. We pack light because we can't see owning a 44-pound 17 foot 9 inch canoe and loading it down with a 46 pound canvas tent. We pack like we're backpacking, and we tend to keep moving in the rain. Also, our tents are made for sleeping and not for group activities, so we'll stay out in a downpour. What we wear *under* the raingear is the key to how much, or how little, we sweat.

Again, we all find poly underwear and fiberpile insulation does the job. There are times in warm, windy rains, when I'd welcome a short *Gore-Tex* jacket without a hood, because it would be more comfortable than the big Peter Storm rain jacket I wear. If it's a really warm rain, I'll paddle in as little as the law allows. And the mosquitos. My skin, after all, is reasonably waterproof, even if it doesn't fit me as well as it used to.

Canoeing is also a sport in which I find the Supersneaker indispensible. If I have to be in and out of the boat a lot, tossing it over beaver dams and such, I may wear an old pair of running shoes, but mostly I'll wear a pair of Nike *Lava Dome* low-cut hiking boots. They dry quickly if my feet get wet, which they often do because I get in my canoe when it's fully in the water, not when it's on the shore, and they have more than enough support for rough portages. The key to living with these boots is a simple one. Carry lots of socks, and dry the wet ones by putting them on top of your pack.

121

Something else nearly indispensible in my canoe is my pair of stretchy tan pants with well-secured pockets and coated nylon knee patches. I prefer to sit in a bucket seat and paddle like the racers do, but sometimes I kneel, and I find myself kneeling around camp, particularly when I'm the chef. These pants are a unique item, available only from Curtis Canoes in Hemlock, New York, or Blackhawk Outfitters, in Janesville, Wisconsin. They're the same pants I wear bird hunting and hiking, too, and they're comfortable to the point of sinfulness. Yes, these shops will mail-order the pants. They're not cheap, but after you wear them for a while, you'd pay twice as much for a replacement pair if you had to.

Hiking and Camping, Cold Weather

You dress for cold weather hiking and camping like you'd dress for cold weather hunting, except you have a few more considerations. The obvious one is that you'll be walking with a heavy pack on your back, which means that even PTFE parkas will not breathe well. In other words, unless you like vapor barrier clothing next to your skin, you'll get your underclothing and perhpas your insulation wet from sweat. This means that you dress minimally, you carry spares of darn nearly everything, and you wear nothing that will absorb sweat. If this sounds like poly and pile, you've been listening.

Once you're in camp, though, and inactive, it's just plain comforting to haul out the heavy-duty parka and put that on over the dry poly shirt and the pile jacket that's already dried in the meantime. It's not impossible to have rain in even very cold weather, but it's unlikely. However snow is still wet, and wetter still around camp. I defy you to pitch a tent or make dinner in the snow without getting wet. A PTFE parka and pants are very nearly mandatory.

Winter camping is pleasant and not at all as dismal as it may sound. It's no place for bozos who don't think, and it's no place to check out gear unless you have a tried-and-true backup for it. We used to test new winter gear, tents and bags in particular, by setting up winter camp out behind the house. Clothing can be tried out on a day trip. If you're not experienced with winter camping—which isn't a bad way to get back into the country where the car hunters never go—the backyard or nearby forest preserve route may well be the best place to start.

Putting It All Together

By now, the message should be obvious. If you're not doing much walking, choose the sturdiest raingear, the most totally impermeable raingear that you can find. If you're working up a sweat, you need not only raingear that can turn rain, but that can breathe a bit as well. And you need to manage your own body by putting on clothing and taking it off as required. The clothing you play with should be of a material, or materials, that retain a vestige of warmth when they're wet, and that dry easily. Your underwear must be of a material that absorbs no moisture. You'll carry a few spare items of clothing in bad weather, but if you choose your gear wisely and wear it wisely, you shouldn't have to use it. Socks, mitts, and a hat are the exceptions. They'll get wet or damp no matter what you do.

If you look over this chapter again, you'll see a few names mentioned consistently. PTFE shell parkas and pants; fiberpile jackets and pants; bunting pants; wool shirts; wool pants; polypropylene underwear in two different weights; heavy-duty PVC-coat raingear.

These are the key items. You can substitute for the heavy-duty PVC raingear if you don't want to own two rainsuits. The PTFE parka and pants will work nicely, and if you use the same raingear for hunting, it's doing double duty. I don't honestly feel that wool is an acceptable substitute for fiberpile, however good it may be. Ultimately, if you're caught between a rock and a hard place, and your insulation, for some reason, gets soaked, pile will dry enough to wear and wool won't. However, if you already have some good woolen gear, don't ditch it. It's still pretty darn good, and it has the added charm of being paid for. However, you might want to nibble at fiberpile by starting with a jacket. I warn you, though; pile clothing is as addictive as a fast canoe or a good fly rod or a well-balanced double.

There is no acceptable substitute for polypropylene underwear if you're active. If you're not working up a sweat, wool is fine. If you are, you need polypropylene. Everything else is for inside wear when you have the thermostat set for 64° F.

So, after all the shouting and all the lecturing and all the options, it turns out that the clothing you need to keep warm and dry really isn't that much. Most of it does double duty, and a lot of it you can even wear to the movies if you so choose.

Granted, some of it is expensive, but all of it is built to last. And all of it is built to do the job for which it's designed. That's the bottom line. None of us really balk at price if the gear is good, because we all know that the cost of a weekend in the field is more than the cost of the gear. It's really the cost, mental and physical, of the week of work that preceded it.

Epilogue:

Ed and Charlie II

When the black four-wheeler swung off the Route 9 exit at 4:30 in the morning on December third, you could bet your last dollar that it was headed for the Black Bear in Pottersville. Why the Black Bear? It's where you catch a second breakfast during deer season. If you're hunting the lower woods, you eat at Potter's, in Warrensburg. It's not an instruction on your big game license, but it might just as well be.

Two stocky, middle-aged men get out of the truck and walk into the diner.

"Hey, Eddie, second breakfast! Good to be back, babe."

"Yeah, you got that right. Place is packed. Woods will be, too."

"Not where we're going. Here, I'll show you. Yes, I'm ready to order. Thanks, Miss. Two over easy, home fries, toast, juice. Orange is fine. Big one, please. Milk. Yeah, coffee too."

"Same for me, Miss, but I'd like the eggs scrambled. Kind of loose, please. Thanks. Now, where we goin', Charlie."

Charlie unfolded the USGS topo map from its plastic folder, spread it on the table, and pointed with the eraser end of a pencil. "Schroon Lake topo. We'll go up to Olmstedville and take Trout Brook Road into where it branches right off to Alder Brook. That shows the road going all the way through to Charley Hill Road up in The Village, but it doesn't. It stops about where it switches back southeast of Merrills Hill. We'll work east across the bog meadow and up to Marsh Pond. If nothing's doing there, we'll work up the trail into the pass between the two little bumps on Hardhack Hill, drop down to the brook again, follow it back, and we'll be at the truck.

"Hmmm. Looks to be four, maybe five miles. That means eight or so, really. Eat up on the hill?"

"Probably. Eat before if you're hungry. There's still open water in there. It's okay to drink, but I'll still take a little bottle just in case. If we eat up on the hill, it'll be dry, and I don't feel like melting snow."

"Yeah. I know it's water, but it always tastes like somebody left a hot iron on a bedsheet too long."

"That's because you don't melt it right."

"C'mon, Charlie. I do most of the time. Sometimes I get in a hurry and don't take the time to pack it down."

The breakfasts came. The men ate slowly, teasing each other about fish lost and bucks missed in the past.

"Charlie, it's been pretty cold. Sure there's water in there?"

"Yeah. We were in last February on snowshoes, just poking around. There was some open water then, and it was cold, believe me. Fun, though. The kids liked it. Wife didn't go. She was skiing."

"Fishing up there?"

"If the beaver have been busy, you can get some squaretails out of Alder. The pond's done for, though, I think. Acid rain. Nothin' there when we went in last summer. Trout Brook was good, though. Real good. Tough fishing, but worth it."

They finished breakfast, climbed back into the four-wheeler, and rolled out toward Olmstedville. The sky was lightening, but the weather report they'd called in for before they left home said that snow was expected later in the day, with stiff north winds accompanying it. The temperature would rise to about 35° F from the 15° F it was now, and fall steadily all afternoon.

When they parked the car, Ed and Charlie kicked off their moccasins, pulled on heavy wool socks over the light socks they were wearing, and put on felt-lined shoepacs. Both men tucked their pantslegs into the boots, and snapped on high gaiters. The snow wasn't deep enough to warrant them, but they might save a bootful of water if they stepped through in the bog meadows. They pulled on heavy mountain parka shells of closely-woven dacron/cotton fabric, heavily treated for water repellency, over their fiberpile sweaters and polypropylene undershirts, and fussed with the mittens strung through the sleeves.

"God, it's like I was in grade school again. Your Mom make you do this, Eddie?"

"Of course. I had to lose a mitten in the woods once to realize how good an idea it was, though. Damn left thumb still is sensitive, and that was close to thirty years ago. Frostbite isn't any fun, buddy."

They pulled on bright orange watch caps, and slid out of the truck. Charlie opened the tailgate, and both men took small rucksacks out.

"Mmmm", Eddie mused as he rummaged through the pack. "Parka, raingear, extra hat—put that in my windshell—mittens can stay, food, stove, pot, potlifter, chow, munchies are in my pocket already, compass, map...got the extra map, Charlie?"

"Yeah. In a Ziploc already, and I marked the declination lines on it for you. You owe me two bucks for the map, and let's see, twenty-seven bucks for my cartography, and three for gas, and eighteen for my general woods sense and good looks, and..."

"For your looks, you owe me a buck eighty."

"...and the Ziploc's on the house."

"Your generosity is overwhelming. Let's boogie."

"Compass?"

"Right where yours is. In the breast pocket."

"Just checking."

"Thanks, Mommy."

They swung their light packs on and cinched up the waistbelts. Except for their wool pants, everything else, including the packs, was bright orange.

"Now I know how a pumpkin feels," Ed grinned. He slid the rifles out of their hard cases, handed one to Charlie, and slid some hulls into his. "Hope the scopes stayed cool enough back there," he mused. "Don't want'em fogging up."

They dropped over the embankment into the fringe of the bog. It was easy walking, but when they turned to cross the bog, it was evident that the ice wouldn't dependably keep them up. They picked their way from hummock to hummock. As they neared the end of the crossing, Charlie broke through.

"Damn," he muttered. "Gaiters saved me. No water in the boot."

"No sweat. You sure? You got extra socks and liners."

"Nope. Don't need 'em."

They moved silently and slowly through the narrow defile between Hardhack Hill and the north shoulder of Pine Hill. There were tracks, but neither man had seen a deer. The snow was beginning to fall, slowly and gently now, in large, puffy flakes. They worked slowly, carefully, stalking the fringes, poking into the narrow north-south cut between Ledge Hill and Pine Hill and back out again, each on his own side of the ridge until they met by the pond. They skirted the eastern edge of the pond and climbed the sharp rise up to Hardhack Hill. Both men unzipped their parkas to the waist and unzipped the fiberpile sweaters underneath.

"Good little up hill, Charlie. Glad I did some hiking this fall."

"Hey, what did I tell you? It helps. And you get to see something every now and then, too."

"Well, I found you that buck during bow season, didn't I? Of course, you missed him, but..."

Charlie spun to his right, looked intently across the ridge, dropped to one knee and fired. "Yeah! Got him! Solid. Let's go; he won't go far."

"Okay! Way to go. Big one?"

"No, Nice. Fat. Good eating deer." They moved off across the ridge. When they arrived at where the deer had been, there was no doubt that it had been solidly hit. They followed the blood trail for less than a hundred yards and found the buck, dead.

By the time they had field-dressed the deer, the snow was falling in earnest, swept along by a harsh, cutting wind. Charlie had pulled his lightweight nylon rain jacket and pants over his clothing to clean the deer, because it would clean up better than his wind parka. Now he took it off, tucked it in a stuff sack in his pack, and put on a warm winter parka filled with *Thinsulate*. Ed, meanwhile, had returned with a stout poplar sapling to string the deer on for the trek to the truck.

"Put on your parka, Ed. Let's eat", said Charlie, and he dug around in Ed's pack for the stove and the pot and the *Mountain House* freeze-dried meals. In less than a minute, the little *Svea 123* stove was roaring under the pot. In five minutes, they were ready to eat. As they ate, they discussed what their plans should be.

"Ed, next time I'm gonna bring me along a full length pad so I can just lie down and snooze after dinner. This little chunk of *Ensolite* keeps my butt warm, but I could really use some serious R-and-R right about now. Been a great day."

"Sure has. You know, going back across the bog meadow's the short way back, but if this snow keeps rolling in, it'll be exposed and we won't have any idea of what's open water and what isn't. Think we should go over the ridge?"

"Lemme think. Looks good on the map. It's a little bit further, by my figuring, but the stream crossing is nothing at all. Then we hit the road. It's not grown over much. You could follow it in a whiteout, just about. Merrill's Hill is just about due west. Close enough for what we need. The trail runs a bit north across some ledges, but the path is open. Or we can cut due west. No, north by west. I'll figure it out. Easy. We hit the top, just where the trail breaks, and we drop straight down to the stream, then head north by west and we pick up the road. Good idea. It's tougher in some ways, but easier in others. Let's clean up and get rolling."

"After some coffee, Charlie."

"Well... why not. We know where we are, we know where we're going, we're comfortable, our bellies are full, and we're prepared.

Hell, we could eat like kings for a few days right now. Sure, let's do it."

They lingered over coffee, chewed up some dried apricots for dessert, packed up their gear, put the litter in a stuff bag, and were ready to roll.

"Time to strip down, Charlie," said Ed as he put his big parka in his pack and put on the shell parka. "Think it's time for the Balaclava, though. It might be nice if that wind's what I think it'll be like across the knob."

"Good idea. Wait up, and I'll get mine."

"I'm not going far with the deer by myself. I'll wait."

They shouldered the deer and moved slowly and steadily up the rise to the pass between the two summits. As they crested out, the wind hit them. "Hmmm. Time for the old parka hood," Charlie shouted. "Blowing pretty fair. I can't even make our Merrills Hills from here."

They dropped down the mountain as planned, with Ed in the lead running a quick, informal compass bearing. The wind scarcely abated when they hit the low-lying land. Ed stopped, scratching his head through the parka hood. "Hey, Charlie, I thought the stream crossing would be a snap. Looks like you had a hyperactive beaver in here, old buddy. That looks like open water to me, and we ain't gonna just step across it."

"Okay", Charlie yelled. "What do you want to do?"

"Let's just walk a field bearing to the left 90° F. until we can cross, cut 90° F back to the right, and turn left 90° F again when the contour feels right. We'll be in the lee of the hill, and the woods ought to be fairly open."

"Yeah. They're not bad. Mostly hardwoods. Sounds good to me."

Three hundred and ten double paces later, after the 90° F turn, Ed and Charlie turned right, crossed Alder Brook below the beaver dam, and followed the bearing until they felt that they were well enough up on the ridge to make intersection with the road inevitable. Then they turned left 90° F and spiraled around the contours at the base of Merrills Hill.

They were moving slowly, hardly enough of a pace to break into a sweat. They stopped several times to watch the bog meadow fill with snow, and to rest. They also stopped once for a drink of water from Ed's water bottle and some more dried fruit. In a half hour they reached the road, turned left, and found the truck ten minutes later.

As they tossed the deer on top of the truck and secured it, Charlie said, "Next week it's your turn, Ed. If it hadn't been for the snow coming early, I think we would have had a pair of bucks today. Smelled right, if you know what I mean."

"Yeah. It would have been nice, but I don't have anything to prove. Besides, if I'd gotten one on the way back, we'd be turning around right now and going back to fetch him. The only problem is that we really shouldn't take the time to grill this one's liver. That'd hit the spot."

"So would coffee and pie at the Black Bear."

"You got that right. Maybe they'd grill up some liver for us. You never know."

It didn't take long to get back to Pottersville and the Black Bear. As they walked in, the waitress asked if they'd had any luck. They smiled, and said that they had. One fat four pointer and a great, delightful day in the woods.

A slim young guy with a beard, who was nursing a cup of coffee at the end of the counter, looked up at them and asked where they'd been hunting. They told him, and introduced themselves. The young guy wiped the mist from the window, and looked out through the snow swirling in the parking lot at the buck on top of the black four-wheeler. He turned to them after a while and said, "Funny thing. I just got back from taking two guys over to Doc's. Names were Ed and Charlie, and they were driving a black four-wheeler like yours. But all they got was hypothermia and frostbite."

"Yeah," said Ed. "You'll have that."

Trail's End:

In from the Cold and Wet

Back in 1974, when I wrote my first book, a fat little paperback on hiking and backpacking called *Movin' Out,* I never dreamed that it would still be in print and thriving eight years later. All I knew was that after a long, long time spent as a writer, the chance to do a book was a tremendous thrill—and the writing of it was a nerve-wracking job of work.

I couldn't resist tagging on a quotation at the close of that book, and I liked it so well I did the same thing when I finished my winter camping book, *Movin' On,* three years later. That's still flourishing, too. And when you're on a roll, stay with it.

The quotation is the ending of Mark Twain's *Huckleberry Finn,* the greatest book on the real and subjective backcountry ever written. It goes like this.

"...and so there ain't nothing more to write about, and I am rotten glad of it, because if I'd a knowed what a trouble it was to make a book I wouldn't a tackled it and aint't agoing to no more. But I reckon I got to light out for the Territory ahead of the rest, because Aunt Sally she's going to adopt me and sivilive me and I can't stand it. I been there before."

May you always have the Territory to light out for. And when you get there, may you be warm and dry.

H.N. R.
Rotterdam Junction, New York

Other Practical Outdoor Books from Stone Wall Press:

Harry Roberts' other books—

Movin' Out: *Equipment & Technique for Hikers*
160 pages, indexed, paperback, $7.95 list

Harry Roberts, editor of *Wilderness Camping,* has written what the International Backpackers Association calls "an excellent, down-to-earth book on backpacking information." This updated edition includes solid advice on boots, clothing, packs, and sleeping bags, as well as techniques for map and compass, eating well, and learning to be at home in a natural environment. Harry's solid, no-nonsense advice is sprinkled throughout.

Movin' On: *Equipment and Techniques for Winter Hikers*
135 pages, illustrated, paperback, $7.95 list

The companion volume to Movin' Out "...sets down a lot of good, common sense advice and he does it in an engaging, unpresumptuous style." This book will get you started on winter backpacking. It's "...full of good advice and useful information. This is a superb book even if you are only thinking about **MAYBE** going winter hiking." *Backpacker.*

Introducing Your Kids to the Outdoors, Revised Edition, Joan Dorsey
144 pages, illustrations, photographs, appendices, paperback, $8.95 list

Taking young kids and infants with you fishing, backpacking, cross-country skiing and bicycling involves special preparation— but the rewards are great! Dorsey carefully outlines what adults must plan for: Food, safety on the trail, equipment that both fits the youngster and serves its purpose. "Highly recommended for its thoroughly sensible, encouraging advice..." *Blair & Ketchum's COUNTRY JOURNAL.*

Enjoying the Active Life After Fifty, Ralph H. Hopp.
Foreward by Arthur S. Leon, MD.
192 pages, Photographs, paperback, $7.95 list

An exercise enthusiast provides older readers basic, practical information for enjoying a wide variety of aerobic sports and recreational activities. Eighteen detailed activities and accompanying illustrations with complete bibliographies of books and magazines. "Activity is the key to health and staying younger. This book is testament to the fact that its philosophy works." *San Francisco Examiner.*

For Hunters & Fisherman—

Goose Hunting, Charles Cadieux
208 pages, photographs, hardcover, $16.95 list

Stories of personal experience, facts about goose management, goose hunting and watching are interwoven to make for an entertaining and informative book. Cadieux has made the outdoors his life—as a game warden, and an outdoors writer. "The author has a way of making his point, instructing his reader, and entertaining him, all at the same time." *Field and Stream.*

All About Varmint Hunting, Nick Sisley
192 pages, photographs, appendices, paperback, $8.95 list

THE comprehensive book on varmint hunting. Everything varmint hunters want or need to know about chuck hunting, varmint rifles, improving accuracy on the range, and more! The nation's number one varmint—the woodchuck—is covered in complete detail. Shotgunning for crows, starlings, and pigeons is also included.

The Sporting Shotgun, Robin Marshall-Ball
A User's Handbook
176 pages, photographs, illustrations, maps, hardcover, $23.95 list

An important international reference to shotgunning in North America, Britain, and Europe. Marshall-Ball gives the shooter a history of shotgunning, the principles of shotgun mechanics, and hints on the points to consider when purchasing a shotgun. Fully illustrated chapters discuss game and distribution throughout North America and Europe. Indexed.

Backpacking for Trout, Bill Cairns
208 pages, photographs, cloth Kivarbound, $16.95

The founder of the famous Orvis Fly Casting School will help you get into remote streams, lakes, and ponds to catch trout. This very practical, informative book includes the latest in equipment and technique along with advice from regional experts and delicious campfire recipes. With an introduction by Lefty Kreh. This book will add a new dimension to your backpacking and fishing pleasure.

Atlantic Surf Fishing, (Revised Edition), Lester Boyd
160 pages, illustrations and photographs, paperback, $8.95

A completely illustrated guide to surf fishing up and down the Atlantic Coast. You'll find where and how to fish along with exciting and often humorous stories. "Les Boyd is a fine writer, a sensitive soul with a sense of humor and a God-given ability to paint pictures with words. Add to this a fine expertise in the art of marine angling and you have a work that is worthy of any surfman's attention." *Salt Water Sportsman.*

For the Forager—
The Natural World Cookbook: *Complete Gourmet Meals from Wild Edibles,* Joe Freitus
301 pages, illustrations, index, hardcover, $25.00 list

Complete and comprehensive, this is a twenty-year collection of proven gourmet recipes for wild plants, fish, fowl, and game. Hundreds of recipes are carefully presented with clear how-to-find illustrations. Freitus has taken up where Euell Gibbons left off. "Everything for the wild foods connoisseur!" *Scott Wildlife News.*

Wild Preserves: *Illustrated Recipes for Over 100 Natural Jams and Jellies,* Joe Freitus
192 pages, illustrations, paperback, $7.95

"A happy combination of plant identification information and recipes makes this book for the pockets of hunters, camera fans, hikers, followers of Euell Gibbons or just the weekend wanderers. Joe Freitus has written the creative canner's bible!" *The Conservationist.*

For the Conservationist—

These are the Endangered, Charles Cadieux
240 pages, photographs, and illustrations by Bob Hines,
clothbound, $16.95 list

A dramatic look at the plight of our endangered wildlife, along
with current legislation and efforts to save them through agencies,
parks, zoos, and organizations. Thoroughly researched, well
written. "...highly recommended for sportsmen, who have a
responsibility to protect wildlife." *Sports Afield.*

Backwoods Ethics: *Environmental Concerns for Hikers and Campers,* Laura and Guy Waterman
192 pages, illustrations, index, paperback, $7.95 list

Noted outdoor magazine columnists shed light on sensitive
environmental issues with neighborly warmth and humor.
"Outdoorsmen and conservationists concerned about the delicate
balance between the use and preservation of our wilderness areas
should find this book of great value." *EnviroSouth.* A valuable
look at how outdoorsmen can individually do something to
prevent further abuse and erosion of the environment. Endorsed
and selected by the American Hiking Society.

Ask for these books at your bookstore or outfitter, or send your
check for the total list amount plus $2.00 (shipping and handling)
to:

STONE WALL PRESS, INC.
1241 30th Street, N.W., Washington, D.C. 20007